WHAT MAKES THIS THE MOST UP-TO-DATE WINE GUIDE YOU CAN SWALLOW?

BECAUSE Gluck is TASTING WINES TWO MONTHS LONGER AND LATER THAN ANYONE ELSE – thanks to state-of-the-art printing technology. WHEN OTHER GUIDES are already PRINTED and on their way to the shops, Gluck is tasting the latest vintages.

'Mr Gluck makes a charming and witty host'

Guardian

'If you are a wine enthusiast whose inclination on finding an exciting bottle is to wish to share it with the world and sing its praises from the rooftops – and many of us are – Malcolm Gluck is your man'

Newcastle Journal

'For a clear and unpretentious guide to what is eminently drinkable on the supermarket shelf, there is none better than Malcolm Gluck's *Superplonk*'

Edinburgh Evening News

Streetplonk 1999

Malcolm Gluck

CORONET BOOKS
Hodder and Stoughton

Copyright © 1998 by Malcolm Gluck

First published in Great Britain as
a Coronet paperback original in 1998

The right of Malcolm Gluck to be identified as the Author of
the Work has been asserted by him in accordance with the
Copyright, Designs and Patents Act 1988.

10 9 8 7 6 5 4 3 2 1

British Library Cataloguing in Publication Data

Gluck, Malcolm
Streetplonk. – 1999
1. Wine and wine making – Great Britain – Guidebooks
I. Title
641.2'2'0296'41

ISBN 0 340 71312 7

Typeset by Palimpsest Book Production Limited,
Polmont, Stirlingshire
Printed and bound in Great Britain

Hodder and Stoughton
A division of Hodder Headline PLC
338 Euston Road
London NW1 3BH

To A. H. for such a great collection of memoirs

'So much wine goes down it, so many millions of words leap over it, how can it rest?'

Sydney Smith on Francis Jeffrey's throat

CONTENTS

INTRODUCTION

Do you believe in romance? Does romance *really* exist?

These are not the same questions of course; for romance is a figment of the imagination and doesn't exist independently of the mind. Nothing possesses the intrinsic quality of romance, *is* romantic; nothing can inspire romantic feelings unless there is human participation. 'Sentimental value' – it merits the quotation marks – is always reckoned to be worth more than that which can be totted up in pounds, shillings and pence (silly me, there I am being romantic – we don't have LSD any more do we?)

Romance is why certain wines cost a great deal more than others. Sentimental, romantic feelings attach to them and so we do not judge such wines by the quality of their liquid impact; we judge them by ethereal factors having no basis in logic, fact, or, often, any actual recognisable feature which impinges on the palate. It is not coincidence that the word 'romance' has many associated meanings, including, of course, that of literary invention or, if you prefer, 'lies'.

The wine scribe has to swallow all sorts of old tripe romantically packaged. The world of wine is awash with romance. It comes in two forms. There is the historical variety which has passed the test of years and is still swallowed eagerly (like: champagne is incomparably the greatest sparkling wine in the world) and there is the subtly insinuating kind which spills out of the mouths of representatives of wine companies and vineyard owners who serve up anything from the preposterous claim well sauced by spicy dubiety to the downright untruth plainly cooked (like: my vineyard site has been chosen by God to make the greatest pinot noir on earth).

When I was young, it is true, I was an out-and-out romantic who felt thrilled to have himself photographed standing beside a roadsign saying 'Volnay' or 'St Emilion 3 kilometres' and I believed all sorts of mythological mumbo-jumbo about various wines and vineyards. Small tracts of soil I was religiously instructed to believe, were sacred places. But since then, having acquired some measure of maturity and, more importantly, readers about whom I worry constantly and whose interests I regard as my primary concern (an interest I interpret as the acquisition of unvarnished wine possessing wonderful fruit and great texture at a very low outlay), it is the liquid in the bottle which nowadays contains all the romance I need; the rest of it is merely the trappings of the designer or the trumpetings of the maker's ego.

It is instructive in the light of the foregoing, therefore, to consider two of my trips to foreign lands last year. They combined the elements which both baffle and confuse the enquiringly minded wine drinker: firstly, the notion of provenance, that is to say the geographical location of a wine as standing for a guarantee of excellence, and, secondly, the concept of modern marketing and design coming to the aid, or the hindrance, of the wine producer in desperate need of a new image. In the first instance, I refer to smart new Chile; in the second, dear old Germany.

Chile has become the darling of the wine media (but not publications like *The Sunday Times* which unsuccessfully tried, earlier this year, to blacken the country's wine industry). I myself have had no qualms in describing the wines as the most straightforwardly elegant for the money in the world and from this generalisation I have inferred that the growing conditions for Chilean grapes must be incomparable. Would this be borne out by visiting the country? Would I find that climate and soil, what the French term when applied to an individual vineyard *terroir*, are indeed the reasons for Chilean excellence – as many Chileans have claimed?

With Germany, my mission was less concerned with the creation of wine as its final dressing up. The Germans, facing their lowest ebb ever in their peacetime UK wine fortunes, need to do something dramatic; but when one's reputation is Wagnerian how convincing is it to suddenly pass oneself off as a Spice Girl?

Chile: '*The country with the world's longest high street, 1875 miles from end to end, with cactus at one end and glaciers at the other.*'

'My thin country' sighed the Chilean poet Neftali Ricardo Reyes Basoalto (who preferred to be known as Pablo Neruda). This elongated elegance makes Chile a paradox. It is *like* every other country in the world and yet *unlike* every other country in the world. It stretches so far that to go from one end to the other is to travel the equivalent of Lagos in Nigeria to Oslo in Norway (2610 miles). At its topmost part it has the world's driest desert; no recorded rain in several hundred years. It has, at the bottom extreme, icebergs. Somewhere between the two it offers the climates of north Africa, Greece, Spain, Sicily and the benign north shore of the Mediterranean. In its long sprawl and 100 mile width it offers, uniquely, something of everything. And down the middle of it runs 1875 miles of Pan-American highway, either side of which lie the vineyards. To travel this highway is to scuttle along an ever-open fairground of screaming bumper-cars and tear-away trucks.

Pedestrians, many of whom live not only either side of the great road (which they must cross on foot) but occasionally in shacks in the middle, are lottery chickens. Lane changing, either to avoid a bunch of homeward bound school children or merely to maintain the driver's adrenalin level, is so frequent and so furious it turns the passenger's stomach. But then Chilean water, as I discovered to my personal cost, also does this very effectively – even when you've tried never to let the stuff touch your lips. ('Whatever you do, Malcolm,' said Ignaccio Recabarren,

Chilean citizen, 'don't touch our water. Clean your teeth in vodka. *Anything*. Just don't put your lips to the water.')

Chilean water begins life as snow-melt from the Andes. It flows into rivers which strive to take it to the Pacific and on the way it moistens the soil. But it can't be water which encourages vines to blossom and bring forth such elegant wines. The idea is laughable. Water and vines are not even necessarily always good friends. Is the soil itself? Could it be the maritime climate? Maybe Chileans possess a secret formula. If so, what was it?

I went to Chile not only to discover what special aspects of *terroir* formed the basis of Chilean wine excellence but also to see if, in some loosely-defined way, I might also gain some insight into why so much European wine from *terroirs* for which legendary greatness is claimed (and indeed widely accepted by so many credulous fools) was so *jejune*. Finally, perhaps, I would be persuaded that in a perfect world, provenance *would* be the guarantor of wine excellence. Grow the grapes in the right place, it is an attractive theory to believe, and the rest isn't a doddle exactly but it is the recipe for greatness. The French, having masterminded this concept, have passed it on to all other wine countries; even Australians are tempted by the idea that the Coonawarra, say, can one day achieve the cachet of the *haut-Medoc*. I am as sceptical of this idea as I am that every Oxford graduate is clever or even especially intelligent.

Chilean grapes are, naturally enough, grown in that part of the country with the Mediterranean meteorology. To the east are the Andes, to the west the Pacific. Two intimidating barriers to any wine pest and a further delightful leavening of an already gorgeous climate by providing maritime breezes, cool nights, and all that mountain water. Chile is the only wine producer of any significance to whom the phylloxera wine pest has never paid a visit. (Though it has not, note, spared her from the incursions of that greedy *parasite du vin* – the wine writer.) As a result of the phylloxera depredations – which one engaging fairytale claims arrived into Europe via American vine cuttings intended for Lord Rothschild's London garden in the middle 1800s –

it was necessary to graft all European vines on to roots that were phylloxera resistant. The pest draws its sustenance from the roots and thereby deprives the vine, eventually, of life. Chile, never having entertained this parasite, has not needed to use grafted root stock. It still grows the descendants of the original vines brought from France and elsewhere in Europe before phylloxera struck. Are we tasting, then, in Chilean cabernets and chardonnays something of the wines our Victorian forebears drank? Possibly. More likely, not. However, what is indisputable is that Chile's wine vines (it has a large market in table grapes also) produce gloriously rich healthy fruit. The climate, of course, is another crucial factor here. Chile's growing season is long and sunny and the grapes, which truly don't have it better anywhere else in the world, can slowly develop complex sugars and acids. This length of growing season, the length of time a vine can be active and busy as well as the time the grapes spend actually hanging on the vine before reaching ripeness, is a crucial factor in wine quality. In England over the past ten years, for example, the increase by three weeks in the length of what we call summer has been of enormous benefit to UK vineyards and is undoubtedly a huge factor in the increase, albeit small and patchy, in the quality of English and Welsh wine (though not one which makes much difference to the UK's position in the league table of the world's wine countries, arrived at by quantity of wine made, where Blighty resides between Egypt and Madagascar).

But of course the UK doesn't get a summer like Chile's. One of Neruda's poems is an ode to the tomato in which 'a sun, fresh, deep, inexhaustible, floods the salads of Chile'. It's a true image of Chilean produce but more especially the potables. The sun is yet another reason why Chilean wine is so toothsome – it never seems to rain during the harvest time. In Europe, late summer/early autumn rain is one of the banes of even the highest rated vineyards. Rain panics growers; fearful of a dilute crop, with watery juice (because the vines suck it up into the fruit), they may pick grapes underripe, adding sugar later to compensate. Italy has declared 1997 to be the best vintage for fifty years. The reason? It did not rain anywhere in Italy during the period leading up to and during the harvest. Chile can boast such dry balminess every year.

Chile's winemakers provide their own reasons for the quality of their wines. We love our fruit more, they say. Ah. Well. Where have we heard that one before? All winemakers *claim* to revere the fruit which goes into their wines. But in Chile they actually do go beyond mere reverence. In Chile the winemakers are *taught* to worship the fruit. The wines which are outstanding, and there are many, share a common theme of beautifully balanced fruitiness whatever the grape variety. They are classy wines made by winemakers who don't impose chemistry. These men and women interpret. It is the way Chile's homegrown winemakers are schooled to operate. Oenology, the science of winemaking, and viticulture, the craft of vinegrowing, are complementary disciplines at the wineries producing the sleekest wines because in order to get an oenology degree at Santiago's wine college, the Catholic University, a student has first to get a degree in viticulture. The extended course takes five years.

Now every winemaker dedicated to making modern wines anywhere in the world will aim to achieve some measure of fruit fidelity. This means, broadly, that what you taste in the grape will find flavourful expression in the finished wine. Wood, alcohol, the nature of the yeast which has initiated the ferment, and other technical and chemical factors will affect and shape this expression but the overall aim is clearly to define the fruit not obscure it (as when, say, winemakers make the wine too woody or too tannic or employ an over-influential yeast).

So. Fruit is the key. But to turn that key – the finesse with which it is handled – requires a devout belief in the fruit's integrity which in some climates winemakers cannot fully accept. Talking to Chilean winemakers, whether Chilean nationals or American and French winemakers working in the country, gives the impression that they would prefer to manipulate the fruit to achieve an effect in the wine rather than fiddle with chemistry in the winery. The French, for example, believe Australian winemakers are chemists. The Australians consider many French winemakers are slaves to peasant traditions of hot winemaking procedures (as opposed to the cool ferments of the New World) and high yields of grapes. The Chilean wine industry as it has developed over the past eighteen years and further transformed itself over the past five years (and is still so transforming itself) is somewhere uniquely between the two.

The first Chilean winemaker I met on my visit was the highly regarded aforementioned Ignaccio Recabarren. A while back, I rated his Casablanca Santa Isabel Estate 1995 as one of the best chardonnays in the world and it was satisfying to sit looking at the very vineyard which produced this sumptuous wine while I tasted it, yet again, along with several other wines of Senor Recabarren's making. It is a superb food partner this wine (roast salmon stuffed with pesto sauce was the dish first cooked in my household to go with it) and it is interesting that its maker, his searching and quite extraordinary amber eyes alive with interest, was as keen to discuss such an aspect of it as he was to reveal the finer points of its manufacture.

'I live in this area for ten years,' he said. 'I taste the grapes all the time. The same sort of flaws you get in the mouth when you taste the grape you get in the finished wines. So grow perfect grapes and let these grapes call the shots. The idea behind all my Casablanca wines is to express fruit – no malo, little wood – typical fruit of the valley.'

'No malo' refers to the secondary fermentation, the so-called malolactic, which all grape juice, either once it is turned into alcohol or sometimes during the alcoholic ferment itself, will go through if it is permitted to do so by the wine maker. In the case of this wine, the malo is prevented from occurring. Malolactic fermentation is what happens when the wine's natural acidity changes from malic, which is sharp and appley, to lactic which is milky and soft. The big buttery flavours of Australian chardonnays for example are due to malolactic fermentations. It is testament to the richness of the Casablanca Valley fruit that it can, with a barrel fermented example like the Santa Isabel estate wine, demonstrate such superbly balanced oleaginous buttery qualities without the need to go to a secondary ferment.

The fruit is indeed calling the shots, most decidedly, but not without that fruit being picked most judiciously. The grapes aren't simply gathered in one harvest. Some vines are permitted to develop very overripe fruit; indeed, the richness of the Santa Isabel wine comes in part from a tiny proportion of the chardonnay grapes in the wine being allowed to develop noble rot, *botrytis cinerea* as it is known. This rot, which creates the super-sweet wines of Sauternes and the Beerenauslesen of Germany, dehydrates the grapes, thus concentrating huge levels of sugar. It was a brilliant move of Senor Recabarren's to let the wine be blended in this way rather than using chemistry in the cellar. It helped to make this particular Chilean wine one of the most talked-about during my trip – even by other winemakers.

One of whom was Maria del Pilar Gonzalez Tamargo. The Santa Carolina winery and cellar in Santiago, first brick put in place in 1875, is where she makes her wines and it is the only old building still standing in this part of Chile's capital city. The roughstone and mortar (mixed with egg whites for greater resilience) has withstood several earthquakes in those years but my Chilean education had not yet embraced tectonic trembling – as it would, disturbingly, before I left the country – and I am whiling away the time before meeting Miss Gonzalez Tamargo, married but preferring to keep her maiden name and known simply as Pilar, in the winery's garden strolling off a colourful lunch consisting of salami, asparagus, tomatoes, palm hearts, and sweetcorn accompanied by a puff-pastrylike bread which her 1996 chardonnay cheerfully matched – rich sip for each rich eclectic bite.

It is late summer (or early autumn since the grape harvest has begun in the hotter vineyards) and yesterday it was 34° in Santiago. Today it is even hotter; the air thick. The flowers seem leaden. The insects buzz sluggishly, as if in treacle. The Andean foothills, the cordilleras lurking eastward over the winery, are just dark shapes of indistinct promise and it is only because I have been told that is where they are that I even look in that direction. The heat haze and the pollution from thousands of cars and trucks, and from the hundreds of caterpillar-coloured, noxiously-fumed buses which infest the roads of the capital, mask the view like gauze.

Pilar arrives, dapper and friendly, single pearl-encrusted ear lobes perfectly balancing her wide smile of welcome. An easy afternoon of work follows: two sauvignon blancs, a chardonnay/semillon blend, four chardonnays, a chenin blanc, a sparkling wine, four merlots, a malbec, four cabernet sauvignons, and two sweet whites made from grapes harvested late, one of which is utterly sublime drunk with one of the fresh peaches which recline, peeled and fresh, on an adjacent plate. Chilean peaches, let me tell you, have a rich ripeness I have never before experienced. I'm beginning to realise, just as I have in other vine-blessed lands, that if you can grow great wine grapes you can grow just about any temperate fruit superbly well.

The tasting ended abruptly when Pilar is called away to handle one of the small emergencies which attend the annual harvesting of grapes and their transformation into wine. I was of no use. Even the most knowledgeable of wine parasites, and I do not count myself amongst such illustrious company, is useless at harvest time. I can only swallow the stuff (hic) and comment. I was driven back to my hotel, the appetite I had thought the lunch had reasonably satiated beginning to reassert itself.

Was the hotel worth eating in? Or should I take a cab downtown (it was too far, ugly, and traffic-treacherous to walk)? The only hotels I tend to eat in – when I have only the resources of my own company upon which to fall back – are small rural Italian or French ones, not twenty floor edifices of glass and steel set in fashionable suburbs of capital cities where the grub tends to be what is called 'international'. But the book I was reading exerted its grip and so I took a chance, avoided any taxi, and ate an excellent hotel meal of stewed baby eels to start and to follow *Kingclip à la plancha con patatas fritas* – which is to say fish and chips. But what fish! What chips!

The fish was like cod in structure but turbot-fleshed, very finely flavoured and firm, and beautifully cooked. The *pommes allumettes* as crunchy as any I've had in a Paris market-workers' hangout. The wine was from Santa Rita, a crisp sauvignon yet also unusually sunny and warm.

Just like the day which greeted me the next morning as I descended to breakfast in the hotel's glass-sided, outdoor elevator. As it slid down, the sun came up out of the mountains as polished and kitsch as a brass gong. To complete this picture all that was needed was a torso, swinging its hammer, and a sign: 'Good morning – courtesy of J. Arthur Rank'.

Certainly I was vividly struck by the wines I tasted that day. My morning was spent with Caliterra, my afternoon with Errazuriz. At both places I enjoyed suavely textured cabernets which Chile seems to produce at a modest price level without seeming to make any effort. It is this quality of easy fruitiness, mingling both soft drinkability with a serious, thought-provokingly complex undertone, which marks out Chilean wine.

'Forward, never stringent, gentle people making gentle wines,' as someone remarked to me as I trod the heat-bowl of the Errazuriz vineyards with American winemaker Ed Flaherty. Ed has made his name in Chile with the Cono Sur wines but now he's pleased to be at Errazuriz. Why? 'Because I can spend more time with the vines here. I can't pick every grape. But I like to feel I know every one.'

Next day I am whisked off to the Valdivieso vineyards in Senor Christian Sotomayor's pick-up truck. It's a Saturday, but it's also harvest time, so there's plenty for me to see. Valdivieso, when we arrive, is a bustling mass of tractors tugging carts filled with grapes and when winemaker Philippe Debrus does find time to show me some of his wines we are accompanied by the regular shrilling of the mobile phone and anxious assistants dropping in. The wines here – and we manage to whip through fourteen before a stuck valve (or somesuch) calls Philippe away – are uniformly elegant and very rich and became two of the smoothest under-a-fiver reds on any UK wine shelf in 1997: the 1996 Cabernet Sauvignon and the 1996 Merlot at the absurd price of £4.29 apiece. It strikes me that Monsieur Debrus might be chased down the main street of any Bordeaux town and proclaimed a traitor were he to return to his native land and publicly announce his allegiance to reds of such succulence, such finesse, such perfect maturity, acid and tannin balance, and such lovely immediacy of fruit. And such cheapness! £4.29 is giving the wine away (comparably drinkable Bordeaux cabernets or merlots of such style, even if such style could be created in France, would cost three or four times as much).

Philippe side-steps my questions about the difference between the fruit in France and fruit in Chile. 'This is a touchy question' is all he will allow though he does admit that 'Chile is not yet a country with very tannic grapes. So the wines have softness, fatness, a good feel in the mouth. We don't have a five year wait for the bottled wine to soften.'

For immediacy and softness, my next winery, Vina La Rosa, provided another benchmark. Here, with polo ponies wandering amongst the vines (an unauthorised breakout I subsequently learned), I met Adolfo Hurtado and his beautiful wife and baby son. Looking a little like an intelligent version of Kevin Webster of *Coronation Street*, Adolfo makes entertaining wines from classic grape varieties. I was delighted to discover here wines of complexity, texture, richness and absurd drinkability and it was only with some effort that I tore myself away in order to make it in time for the next vineyard on my schedule, Mont Gras.

Here, the energetic Senor Hernan Gras, not only winemaker but the company's managing director, makes a range of wines characterised by a distinctive depth of tone. I tackled here both tank samples and barrel samples, '97 chardonnays predominating, and the most interesting thing was the difference between the barrelled wine (with woodiness in a two week-old wine already a presence) and the tank samples of wines made from vines which were drastically pruned of half their fruit four weeks prior to harvest. The wine in this instance was sensorily more concentrated and less obvious. This would provide more complex wine in the end because of greater development potential in the bottle as it aged. This might not necessarily be true of the wood matured wine in spite of the added complexity which the wood ought to bequeath. More evidence of the high quality of the initial grapes? Testimony to provenance? I am not so sure. I felt the weighty richness of the wines reflected the weighty richness and personality of their maker (romantic twaddle maybe, but that's what struck me).

One of the most vivacious of Senor Gras' already fully mature wines, Mont Gras Cabernet Sauvignon Reserva 1996, is a snip under six quid. It has a deep weight of fruit, it literally piles itself on to the taste buds like a rich jammy spread, but it is, in fact, a dry wine which goes very well with food.

Overall, however, this is not true of a great many Chilean reds. They lack the muscularity (unlike, say, a southern Rhone, or a rustic Chianti, or certain Spanish reds) to tackle really robust food. The whites, curiously, are big enough to tackle richly flavoured fish dishes but the reds need careful partnering.

After this I was off to a winery I had never before heard of until I came to Chile. But Jane Cresswell, export director of this unknown quantity, Vina Bisquertt, went to great lengths to help me during my stay in the country and so I was alerted immediately to the civilised idea that Bisquertt was keen to make an impression. It had, it seemed, not made much of one before with its wines and it was interesting to discover why. The fruit had been of a decent quality but the wine making had not been as modern and as skilled as it could have been. Tasting a Chardonnay 1996, a La Joya Chardonnay Gran Reserva 1996, a Sauvignon Blanc 1996, a Cabernet Sauvignon 1995, a La Joya Cabernet Sauvignon Gran Reserva 1994, a Merlot 1995, a La Joya Merlot Gran Reserva 1995, admittedly making allowances for a tasting room which had a most unpleasant ratty odour, I was unable to rate any wine greater than 13.5 points. I also tasted some wines in tank, as well as some in the local beech wood called rauli. I found the latter very harsh and unkind to the fruit.

But then I met Englishman David Cowderoy, ex-Roseworthy (Australian wine university) graduate and who has previously worked for BRL Hardy in Adelaide, on loan from Tenterden vineyards in Kent, whom Bisquertt had hired on a three-month contract to vinify 50,000 cases of 1997 wine for England. I was fascinated by his use of tannin powder in a white wine and enthralled by his conversation in which enzymes, yeasts, and various must treatments figured largely. He will undoubtedly improve the Bisquertt wines; thus strengthening the proposition that the individual making the wine has more say over its quality than the grapes – however good they might be.

Next day I uncovered more evidence of this at Vina Viu Manent which though it sells table grapes to Sainsbury and Safeway does not yet sell them any wines. The *Sunday Times* Wine Club is the place, or rather the mail order company, which, so I was told, sells some of the stuff I tasted: Viu Manent Merlot 1996, Viu Manent Malbec Reserve 1996, Viu Manent Cabernet Sauvignon 1995, and Hacienda San Coplos Cabernet Sauvignon 1995. The two most interesting reds were Viu Malbec 1996, which might be on sale in UK, which I rated 15 points, and Viu Manent Cabernet Sauvignon Reserve 1994. This last managed only a 13 point rating on my scale of values but the interest was the extraordinary aroma. I was told: 'It's supposed to be like a French wine's smell. French Cabernet Sauvignon. We wanted native yeast to give it this bouquet, so 30% of the wine was fermented using native yeast, the rest using a yeast called F10.' On the basis of this, it was plain to me why modern new-world winemakers prefer selected yeasts, with which they innoculate the grape juice, over which they have complete control and whose characteristics are fully known. It is yeast which turns sugar into alcohol and grapes attract yeast on their skins, like vultures to an expiring beast; but the modern trend is towards the use of yeasts developed outside the winery and available commercially. Not very romantic, but more efficient and predictable.

More soothing to my palate were Manent's whites: San Carlos de Cunaco Sauvignon Blanc/Semillon 1995 which I rated as high as 15-points at a projected retailer price of a fiver, Viu Manent Sauvignon Blanc 1996 which it was hoped Oddbins might take but which I could rate no higher than 13.5, Hacienda San Coplos Chardonnay and Semillon 1996 (rating 13.5) which was expected to sell for around £6/£7 in UK mail order outlets, and Viu Manent Chardonnay 1996 which is only sold in Chilean restaurants and supermarkets.

Over a lunch of boiled beef and avocado under a lemon tree, someone said: 'Every oenologist in Chile has to be an agronomist first. Not like that in France.' Well, that's good to hear. And certainly some of the cabernet vines I saw at Viu Manent looked in superb condition, testaments to conscientious agronomy. They were at the peak of maturity, too, at 40 years-old. The yield of some of them was twelve tons of grapes per acre. Overall, though, I was disappointed. The wines weren't as concentrated, as simply thrilling, as I've been used to with Chilean fruit. They could have been better. None of the wines here seemed to me in Chile's first rank.

In contrast, my next winery was, if my ratings are anything to go by, at the very top: Casa Lapostolle. Now it is only fair that you should know how I was feeling by this stage of my trip. I'd been at it nine days or so. I was missing my wife, my children, my computer, the inanities of the Tory party (this was several weeks before Labour's stunning result swept them from power), and I was feeling, unusually for me, lonely and disconnected. I was, then, exceedingly well knackered before I visited the winery – at which Michel Rolland is a consultant – and tasted the Casa Laspostolle wines. But it is another Michel, Michel Friou, who makes the wines and whose wines, wearily, I began to taste.

But wow! Frankenstein's monster has come to life. The wine parasite twitches with delight and energy!!! This is what brilliant wine does for the dying. It brings them to their senses. Who is

Michel Rolland you ask? He is to parts of Bordeaux what Eric Cantona was once to Manchester United football club.

Overall: these are stunning wines making vivid statements but doing it in quiet, measured, eloquent tones of precision and poise. Casa Laspostolle makes a range of wines of nobility of fruit, elegance of stature, varietally beautiful, decisively charming, complex yet immediate. It is one of the most tightly focussed – to use a somewhat horrid but current buzzword beloved, I have noted, of mobile phone fans – wineries in Chile. Indeed, it is a winery which is first class *plus* – yet it is big enough and commercial enough to turn out 130,000 cases a year. The Rapel Valley, where Casa Lapostolle is situated, is patently, on this evidence, a great wine area of the 21st century. (Ah! Provenance is creeping back on the agenda.)

Nevertheless, in spite of the immense charm of the wines and the immense eloquence of Monsieur Friou, I felt the need to speak to my wife and children. I proceeded, over the next hour whilst M. Friou was called away on some minor *crise de recolte*, to make three phone calls to my wife's answerphone. In response I get the voice I hate most in the world. I know that the family cannot possibly guess that I will telephone them from a valley in Chile at 8.29 in the evening UK time but still that formal, peremptory 'leave a message after the tone' android tonality is worse than a phone which rings unanswered. It makes me feel more lost and greatly unloved. I feel exhausted now – drained of the will to sip any more wines. With luck I'll only be invited to *swallow* them.

Michel returns from his crisis and we drive out into a vineyard still awaiting the pickers. We stroll around and taste the grapes, yet to be harvested. Michel tells me about how the legendary Michel Rolland's Bordeaux ideas work in the Rapel. 'Michel has taught us not to pick by the dictates of the laboratory but by the grapes' skins. The tannins must be soft, not green.'

But isn't this what all new world winemakers do? Australians will surely only go by what they taste in the grape rather than what some lab instrument tells them? Michel chooses the words for his reply with precision as I chew on his fruit.

'Aussies will pick when the grapes seem ripe to taste but only do so when lab analysis confirm sugar and acid. Michel taught us that the secret is not in the pulp but the skins. The tannin is here. This merlot here seems ripe but it needs two weeks more. The tannins are green. An Aussie would be frightened of Ph and sugar in the lab and pick them. We do not. We wait until our tastebuds tell us the tannins are ripe and soft.'

How often does Michel's namesake fly over from Bordeaux and monitor progress? 'He's closely involved five weeks a year. He makes five visits.'

I feel I'm getting close, at last, to the secret of Chilean wine quality. The people who make the best wines simply know what they're doing and one prerequisite of such an attitude is an insistence on growing the best grapes. It's easy, no? But let the wines speak for themselves. These are the ratings of the wines I tasted with Michel Friou:

Casa Lapostolle Sauvignon 1996 17-points (£4.99 in UK), Casa Lapostolle Chardonnay 1995 18-points (£6.49 in UK), Casa Lapostolle Cabernet Sauvignon 1995 16-points (£6.99 if it gets to the UK), Casa Lapostolle Cabernet Sauvignon Cuvee Alexandre 1995 17.5-points (very little on sale in the UK), Casa Lapostolle Merlot Cuvee Alexandre 1995 18-points (was around nine quid at Safeway and the Wine Society).

Is the secret in the skin? All that deep lush tannin? Or is it in the depth of the mind of the man who can appreciate these things? I repair to the Rabat family hacienda for the night, guest of the winery, and contemplate these matters. But not before I have a supper of more avocados. The tomato salad, when I spotted it earlier prior to eating, seemed gratifyingly decorated with generous shreds of black pepper; when I examined the salad at close quarters ten thousand tiny flies departed it in a black cloud. It was difficult to eat that salad at supper. Maybe flies are considered a delicacy in Chile. Maybe what I ate at supper was fresh fly salad with tomato on the side. My stomach feels queasy all night. This poor gringo among the grapes is beginning to feel even more stressed.

Having slept in the Rabat family hacienda, endured a break-fast of further fly-bestrewn fruit and enjoyed instant coffee from a thermos flask, I sit on the verandah of the hacienda and contemplate Chile and, I hope, the imminent arrival of a man from the Luis Felipe Edwards winery to whisk me off to taste wines, gaze at stainless steel and admire vines. A wine trip centres around the latter three phenomena. You can either learn nothing new from each experience or one of them might provide an important clue to the mystery of wine. My mystery is hanging on the vines: why are these grapes making such remarkably elegant and balanced wines?

The answer is, obviously, in the nature of the grapes Chile grows *and* how these grapes are treated when picked. In other words, Chile is no different from anywhere else in the world which makes wine. Why do I bother to travel anywhere?

But also consider these elements: ungrafted rootstock, long dry summers with no rain during harvest, extended grape hang, deep respect among growers for fruit quality, new world viticultural and wine making techniques, maritime climate providing cool nights (to build up acids) to balance the hot days (which concentrate the sugar in the grapes). The answer is in there somewhere.

Finally, amidst all this musing, a pick up truck arrives to whisk me off to meet Senor Edwards in Colchagua. In his tan slacks, blue short-sleeved polo shirt, generous hint of Surrey jowl, grey thinning hair cut in the style favoured by successful City insurance agents, and immensely jocular disposition, Senor Edwards, a Chilean to his fingertips, is every bit, it seems to me, the issue of his British ancestors who came over to Chile when Victoria was still getting to grips with being a queen.

He's very proud of his table grape set-up. I see grapes packed with protective treated paper to preserve them on their long sea-journey go straight into the cold room to await the truck (also refrigerated). So, I learn something else: these guys were into refrigerated treatment of fruit way back – long before it became *de rigueur* for wineries anxious to be considered fashionable and modern. The grapes are on their way to Tesco – along with some of the wine which Fullers, Oddbins, and Majestic, so I'm told, are also keen to get their hands on.

The ratings of these wines, as with Casa Lapostolle, says it all: Chardonnay 1994 16.5-points (£3.99), Pupilla Cabernet Sauvignon 1996 16.5-points (£3.99/£4.20), Cabernet Sauvignon 1995 15-points (£4.99), Reserva Cabernet Sauvignon 1995 16-points (£5.99 to £6.20). The Reserva Cabernet Sauvignon '96, tasted on a cold January 1998 afternoon in London, was as as good as the '95 and hugely warming.

Naturally, I tour the vines, chew some fruit (including some wild figs which helped alleviate the effect of all those squashed flies), and then I was invited to lunch at Hacienda Luis Felipe Edwards where as a tidbit, sitting on the verandah where the rose bushes fringe the swimming pool, the high hills overshadow the poplars, and chickens peck amongst the grass on the lawn, I was offered six-hour old cow's cheese with green chillis – and finally those flies began to fade. What a lovely location in which to sip the '94 chardonnay from this estate. It is amongst the most delicate and lemony of Chilean chardonnays.

Lunch consisted of avocados stuffed with tuna, chicken with wild mushrooms and prunes, home-made butter so rich it made the bread groan, and watermelon which tasted of melon rather than water. So. Even the watermelon in Chile is extraordinarily fruity.

At 4.20, lunch still a delicious memory (flies finally undone and flown), I was driven away to meet Senor Aurelio Montes, whose second name is to be found on many bottles on UK wine shelves (as Montes, Villa Montes, and Montes Alpha, as well as an own-label *Sunday Times* Wine Club wine). He makes wines, under the name Discover Wines, in Curico and the first thing this Viking-looking man with teeth like a chain-saw told me was that it was 34.8 degrees in the vineyard yesterday and the grapes are still coming in. In spite of being in the middle of the hustle and bustle of grape delivery and first pressing, Aurelio found time to produce glasses of new '97 wines, middle ferment liquid, from the tanks of chardonnay and sauvignon blanc. This was from very ripe fruit but the potential for complexity as a developed wine seemed to me considerable. I also tasted Merlot '97 after only four days in its fermenting tank and was astonished at the forwardness of the fruit. Even more astonishing was Aurelio telling me that the yield of the vineyard was a mere 2 tons an acre because it was such a new vineyard, still a long way from maturity when its yield would be five times that at least.

The best wine here though, naturally enough, was a matured specimen, a '96 which was being transferred from its barrels to bottles where it will stay for some months before being sold. This was 1996 Montes Alpha Chardonnay and I felt it had a rich and exciting future ahead of it. But perhaps I learned more about Chilean fruit when I enjoyed a short tea-break at the homestead, just along from the winery. Tea came with the thickest, richest, most perfumed blackcurrant jam I've ever tasted and I was presented with a jar to take home (which unfortunately got left behind in a motel – I stowed it away in the corner of a cupboard to keep hidden from flies and . . .).

The Chilean landowning class, on the evidence of the wealthy farmer/wine grower, is very suburban in spirit and is furnished with ideas of similar ken. The men are a trifle soppy, not all agricultural in either gait or gaiters; pleased to press upon you their enthusiasms and they have a sweetness of disposition so English that it is no surprise to learn that other south Americans call the Chileans the English of the sub-continent. I can imagine the horror, the sheer stiff-upper-lip-clenching horror born of bafflement and helpless rage, which visited some of these families when at the beginning of the Allende revolution some of their workers and local peasants, having been invited to think along anarchic lines, simply marched into certain haciendas and took over – lock, stock, and barrels of wine.

Interestingly, I did not meet a single one of these usurpers during my visit. No-one could give me a credible explanation of what happened to them but then I was hardly here to press this point; however, press it I would have felt compelled to do had I not decided, that very day, to cut my visit short. I was simply exhausted from all the travelling up and down the Pan-American highway by high speed car; however congenial the driver, I was dead on my feet.

It was March the 13th the next day. A good day to finish and talk to the man who was the overseas pioneer of Chilean vineyard management and wine production: Miguel Torres, also of Catalonia and California. Miguel, I think I know him well enough now to call him that (besides, I've promised him tennis lessons next time I get to Barcelona), first came here in 1978. 'What impressed me, you know, was that from Spring to the Fall no rain fell. This was a great climate in which to grow superb, healthy vines and produce complex wine.' In January 1979 he bought the estate in Curico, the Maquehua bodega and 250 acres of vineyard from the Ahrex family (who surely must be kicking themselves now), and this acquisition without question was a milestone in the history of the Chilean wine industry. It has been the equivalent, if I may stretch FIFA rules to breaking point, of Manchester United buying a fourth division club in Sicily and turning it into a Serie A member with the clout to challenge Juventus.

What did he think of my theory about ungrafted vine roots being the basis of Chilean wine quality? He pooh-poohed it. He was polite. Miguel is always polite. Climate yes. Maritime cold air at night and a long hot summer oh yes. Oh yes. He went along with everything. But ungrafted vine roots? Maybe if I was in his position I wouldn't go along with the idea either; after all, it damns all the vines in Europe, including his own, as being sub-standard. I scribbled my notes and went into tasting-bout mode. (But not before another Chilean mystery which had been bugging me was cleared up by the polymath the other side of the tasting table. Why, I wanted to know, were Chileans so fond of drinking instant coffee? This was south America wasn't it? Why couldn't I get a decent expresso anywhere? 'Chileans love Nescafe. The factory here produces a unique blend of it. Some tourists take Nescafe home as a souvenir. Nescafe is even available in pharmacies in Chile. The only country in the world where this is the case.' For nervous tension perhaps? To relax all the surviving maniacs on the highway?)

I was keen to meet Senorita Torres, Miguel's daughter, but didn't. She's finished a chemistry and oenology degree at Montpelier and is in Chile involved in her very first vintage of making her own wine. But a few tons of grapes were exercising her attention and she would only be free later, when I would be on the road to Santiago, to fly home the next day.

Miguel takes me through a tasting of his Chilean wines. Each has the Torres hallmark, which is to say of a wine it has balance, restraint rather than full-bloodied fruitiness, and is not aggressively modern in feel (though thoroughly modern in manufacture). There is always with a Torres wine, even with the most expensive and richly flavoured, a sense of mannerly civility; as if the wine makes a little bow from the waist or a curtsey from the knees before shyly getting to grips with the palate and this is, of course, not the modern way at all. Australia has taught many wine makers that primary sensation is everything. It isn't, but it does leave many pioneering spirits like Miguel Torres – who ventured in to Chile before the crowd did and was the first to introduce stainless steel and cold fermentation techniques into Spain – seeming to be old-fashioned. However, I believe that even the largest wine concern (or any commercial undertaking for that matter), if it is under the aegis of a talented, energetic, visionary individual, will take on aspects of that individual's personality and style. The soul of the inspiring spirit imbues the company; and with Torres this is true whether the wine is made in Catalonia or Curico. Even in California, completing an agreeably alliterative line-up, where an equally strong-minded Torres, Miguel's sister Miramar, runs the vineyard, the chardonnay and pinot noir, often outstanding examples of these grape varieties which comfortably put *soi-disant* world-renowned Cote d'Or vineyards growing the same grapes to shame, there is a sense of this calm restraint and refusal to show-off, flaunt the fruit for the sake of it, and be flamboyant.

Of the wines I tasted this day, the Manso de Velasco Cabernet Sauvignon 1994, made from a special block of very old vines, was the most exuberant and insistent. This lovely cabernet, which will develop impressively in bottle for anything up to seven years, rates 16 points and costs around £13 in the UK from the few small wine merchants which stock it (put that in the past tense – it's surely all been sold by now). Not much more than 300 six-bottle cases end up for sale in Britain. In fact, Torres prefers as a company to trade with small merchants rather than the major wine shops and supermarkets.

The other Torres wines I tasted were Santa Digna Chardonnay 1996 (15.5-points, around £5) which is over 90% fermented in new French oak from the Nevers forest and has 100% malolactic fermentation. It is the percentage degree of this transformation, which skilled winemakers know precisely how to control each harvest, which determines the final style of the wine. Often the final bottled wine is a blend of barrels where full malo has taken place and barrels where none has taken place. This blending is another aspect of the craft of wine making.

Don Miguel Riesling y Gewurztraminer 1996 rated 16 points, Cabernet Sauvignon Rose 1996 rated 16, Santa Digna Sauvignon Blanc 1996 was a 15-pointer, Bellaterra Sauvignon Blanc 1996 rated 13, an experimental 1995 Syrah 1995 not yet in commercial production I didn't rate, Santa Digna Cabernet Sauvignon 1995 rated 15.5, an experimental sweet riesling 1996 wasn't rated, and equally I didn't rate the sparkling Miguel Torres Brut Nature 1995. Let me point out that the phrase 'didn't rate' does not mean the wine was poor; it means the wine cannot be rated by my habitual system because this incorporates a value-for-money consideration and so with a non-commercial wine or a wine not available in the UK rating points do not apply. The syrah and the sparkling wine, the '96 of which is now coming on to the English market and which vintage I have not tasted, were both excellent.

However much I tried to press the idea, Miguel wouldn't buy the notion that Chile's wine quality is due to ungrafted rootstock; but he did concede that growing conditions were so outstanding that insecticides and herbicides widely in use in Europe are in minimal use in many Chilean vineyards. He told me how they had learned to deal with the dreaded red spider, a vine parasite, which involved 'insecticide restraint'. He went on: 'We let the spider do its worst. Its predators increase and they get rid of it. If you spray insecticides, you remove all the predators and next year the spider is back with a vengeance.' (When, many months later, I talked to an analytical chemist about pesticide levels in Chilean wine, inspired to do so by the report in *The Sunday Times* on the subject I was told 'Pesticide levels in Chilean wine? Chile comes out squeaky clean in all my tests.')

Miguel Torres also left me with the sobering consideration that 'We are discussing suing three cork producers at present.' It is not my intention to go into cork taint in this introduction, readers may well be sick and tired at my ceaseless sounding off about it, but it is interesting how wine companies world-wide are at last beginning to apply pressure on cork producers to clean up their acts.

The last winery I was able to visit on my trip was San Pedro, which can date its birth as far back as the historic year of 1701 (not a lot happened in Chile that year but as every schoolboy knows it was the momentous year the British parliament passed the Act of Settlement confirming the accession, when the childless catholic Queen Anne died, of the Protestant Hanoverians who managed four Georges, a William, and a Victoria). Historically, San Pedro is significant, however, for as long ago as 1907 it installed the first cold treatment facility for wine in the world. Today, modernity, after many years of muddling and mediocrity, is once more the keynote and it was here I met Jacques Lurton (not for the first time) who is consultant to the winery. I also met resident Lurton team-member, Brett Jackson, who is based at the winery and responsible for wine making day to day.

He confirmed my growing conviction that climatically Chile doesn't lag behind anyone or anywhere else on the planet in offering grapes heavenly growing conditions – including Brett's native New Zealand. I was certainly very impressed with the sauvignon blancs I tasted here, the excellent cabernets and a very good merlot. Prices are reasonable here, too; but then with two and half thousand acres of their vines, San Pedro has exclusive access to its own fruit.

After some of the previous stomach-churning experiences I had endured being driven on the Pan-American highway, it was agreeable to potter back to Santiago on this road and feel comparatively relaxed sitting beside Maria Claudia del Fierro at the wheel. When she told me of her own near-fatal crash on this very road, I felt pleased this was my last trip on it. 'What you have to understand, Malcolm,' she said, 'is that in Chile a driver sees his honour at stake if he doesn't overtake a car which is indicating to change lanes. So: no-one indicates when they change lanes.'

'You do,' I pointed out.

She shrugged. She was a woman.

One with a strong stomach I noted later when I enjoyed a farewell dinner of Mexican food, plenty chillies, at the restaurant where Jancis Robinson once had her handbag nicked. Later, I discovered it was a restaurant which specialised in theft. The chillies robbed me of a night's sleep.

But then an earthquake tremor also contributed to that loss. That, and the fact that in spite of observing Senor Recabarren's stricture to avoid the tap water, some had entered my system and I was finally struck down by one of those unmentionable intestinal conditions which render even bottled mineral water a prickly prospect to swallow.

When I landed at Heathrow the next day, I was a wreck. But in my shoulder bag, in my messy, bulging, rubber-banded notebooks, I had confirmation of what I had always suspected: provenance, vineyard site as a guarantor of quality, is meaningful *only if the wine maker knows what he is doing*. Yes, quite patently, many vineyards in Chile enjoy uniquely magnificent growing conditions but not all of them can create wonderful wine as a result. How could this question be answered any other way?

What makes Chilean wine so superb? The wine makers. That's the answer. Put the question another way and you get the same answer. What makes certain wines from famous sites indifferent? The wine makers (plus the vine growers in many instances, which may be one and the same person). I must add to this my belief that consistent dry weather conditions at harvest makes Chilean grapes extra-special any way.

Travel to Germany, however, and we are back once again in the land of The Revered Site. The Germans worship pieces of vineyard soil even more than the French, perhaps because the most revered are almost invariably in spectacular, vertiginous, naturally awe-inspiring positions whereas even the greatest of the French are merely on hillocks. Germans are also attracted to the idea of the individual person being subsumed under the greater genius of a grouping or a magnetic idea. Even Goethe and Wagner, massive individual personalities, are referred to via some sort of philosophical conceptualising which has its followers, a group of adherents. Even militarily, the names of groups, Teutonic Knights, SS, Panzers, are more powerful names than any individual's (Rommel's, perhaps, apart in this century). Of course, Germans have heroes and even heroines, but they are romantic ones; quasi-religious awe is reserved for the Doctor vineyard, for example, but which maker of any of this vineyard's wines carries the same halo?

By the same token, the Germans don't find individuals funny except in an embarrassing or hilarious situation. In this context, it is true to say that everything I saw in my last trip to this country gave the lie to the widely held belief that the Germans do not *possess* a sense of humour in the first place. Unless, that is, you're going to tell me they're *serious* about a wine which comes in plain glass bottle with a twisted neck called Bend in the River. This is, however, the latest twist in the history of German wine.

The complete history of German wine has yet to be written. Already you yawn. The prospect is hardly as intimidatingly delicious as the thought of the next Ruth Rendell or even, to plumb the least complex and most thickly pureed depths of digestibility, as approachable as any forthcoming Jeffrey Archer. Yet German wine, as much as French, has figured greatly in the literature of Europe and for some reason its most glorious appearances never make the pages of those ghastly literary anthologies, compiled by people who really ought to be better employed, which offer snippets from novels and biographies in which wine (more often it is food) features. It seems either that these compilers are so poorly read they are ignorant or they pass over German characterisation as too unsightly or soppy for readers. This is perhaps because German wine, presenting the opposite image of its national image (butch and brainy), is seen as 'feminine', flowery, witless and insubstantial (i.e. not alcoholic enough). George Meredith, whom it is true *nobody* loves and reads any more (and arguably no reader did love when he was alive and scribbling), is a typical example of a writer using German wine as some sort of backdrop for sodden romanticism. This may have some basis in actuality, since we know Germans are a desperately romantic people (otherwise they would have simply ridiculed National Socialism as hollow opportunism and laughed Hitler out of politics before either became a force for practical evil). Meredith's novel *The Tragic Comedians*, to be recommended to any modern reader no further than its opening paragraph which contains a striking metaphor for Human Nature likened to a wandering ship with a mutinous crew, a drunken pilot, and a mad captain, has, as this preposterous melodrama develops, Chlotilde von Rudiger and her would-be lover Alvan drinking Rhine wine. Alvan refers to the raisins which German wine growers employ to make what he, erroneously via Meredith's mistaken ideas, refers to as 'that copy of the French sauternes'. It is more likely that the French copied German trockenbeerenauslesen than the other way around. Indeed, the Germans followed the Hungarians, who had their intensely sweet wine Tokay up and running (slowly) two centuries at least before the Rhinelanders discovered it, and the Hungarians merely did what the Romans had known about centuries before – letting certain grapes hang on the vine until November when they became shrivelled, dehydrated, and were concentrated with high levels of sugar. The point here, however, is that the characters get worked up about the Rhine grape, in its youngest and least sweet form, and, in Meredith's cloying prose, even propose basing some of their future happiness on the contents of a wine cellar. Could any character in a modern novel get so worked about German wine? What I am driving at here is that German wine was once seen as the greatest on the planet; modern developments should be seen in this context.

In numerous instances of 18th and 19th century writing, particularly the latter century, we gain an insight into just how greatly admired German wine was in those days and what manner of wine it was which wine drinkers (exclusively gentry as far as non-native drinkers of German wine went) enjoyed. The memoirs of the great Russian thinker Alexander Herzen give us an accurate insight into how prized such wine was (in the 1830s and right up until the beginning of the First World War) and of the kind of style German wine took in those hey-days. Herzen has been exiled by the Tsar. He writes: 'Ten days after my arrest a little swarthy, pock-marked policeman appeared some time after nine in the evening with an order for me to dress and set off to the commission of inquiry. While I was dressing the following ludicrously vexatious incident occurred. My dinner was being sent me from home. A servant gave it to the non-commissioned officer on duty below and he sent it up to me by a soldier. It was permitted to let in for me from home half a bottle to a whole bottle of wine a day. N. Sazonov took advantage of this permission to send me a bottle of excellent Johannisberg. The soldier and I ingeniously uncorked the bottle with two nails; one could smell the bouquet some distance away. I looked forward to enjoying it for the next three or four days.

'One must be in prison to know how much childishness

remains in a man and what comfort can be found in trifles, from a bottle of wine to a trick at the expense of one's guard.

'The pock-marked policeman sniffed out my bottle and, turning to me, asked permission to taste a little. I was vexed; however, I said that I should be delighted. I had no wine-glass. The monster took a tumbler, filled it incredibly full and drank it down without taking breath; this way of pouring down spirits and wine only exists among Russians and Poles; in the whole of Europe I have seen no other people empty a tumbler at a gulp, or who could toss off a wine-glassful. To make the loss of the wine still more bitter, the pock-marked policeman wiped his lips with a snuffy blue handkerchief, adding "First-class Madeira". I looked at him with hatred and spitefully rejoiced that he had not been vaccinated and nature had not spared him the smallpox.' (*My Past and Thoughts: The Memoirs of Alexander Herzen*, revised by Humphrey Higgins, published by Chatto & Windus, 1968)

The sweet tooth of 19th century Russian gentry and aristocracy is well known, but Herzen's description is an interesting clue as to the precise style of the German version of it. German wine, as drunk in those days, was obviously old, honeyed, highly perfumed, extremely unctuous, and a little went a long way. It was also, I believe, very complex and saved from simple sweetness by virtue of its huge acidity which carried a unique mineralised edge. It was this balance of fruit and acid which gave it such a long life, both in bottle *and* once opened – Herzen looked forward to drinking it over several days remember. The wine was, then, no different from a mature great single estate beerenauslese of today. Johannisberg was a revered site then and it is still today since the area was first planted with vines soon after Charlemagne's death in the early ninth century.

The popularity of German wine did wane after 1919 but since there was no-one around to take advantage of Germany's somewhat tarnished reputation, German rieslings did not go completely out of fashion. The sheer lunatic policies of the military geniuses running the First World War, who failed to save from the slaughter the future vignerons of so many French vineyards meant that France had significant areas under vine which became neglected and forgotten – or were replanted with easier crops than the labour-intensive grape. By the end of the 1945 war many wine drinkers had had their fill of German wine and though Blue Nun, created as a brand of Liebfraumilch in the 1920s, did corner a profitable chunk of the market, in general the notion of German wine as the handcrafted product of individual estates, as wine to lay down for years, languished both because of the tainted image of Germany and the social revolution which saw the end of the cellar, the downstairs maid, and the butler. What was Germany to do?

It simply, according to one theory, went the way German ingenuity meets every crisis – it re-engineered itself and became more straightforwardly sweeter, cheaper, immediately drinkable, and attractive to American GIs who also drank sweet cola. These factors, with the help of the introduction of some barmily dilutory and standard-weakening German wine laws enacted in the 1970s, have all helped the German wine industry to find itself in a weakened position, unable fully to meet the challenges of the wine revolution in the UK which took place over the 1980s and 1990s.

Yet even as recently as 1993 just over 24% of all wines sold in this country came from Germany. Four years later, by 1997, this had shrunk to just under 15%. This is an extravagant fall in popularity and it dramatically consolidates the lead of the French, the Italians and the Spaniards in their wine exports. It is illuminating in this regard to look at the UK's second largest wine merchant here, J Sainsbury. This supermarket currently carries 28 different German wines on its shelves. However, incredibly, there are 44 South Africans. This is a measure of how much impact the New World of wine has had on the Old.

To arrest the decline, the German authorities conceived a brilliant solution. They would sponsor a wine tasting competition in the *Radio Times*, ask me to decide the finalists, and then fly us to Germany for a few days to consume personally all the wine which was no longer finding its way to Britain.

What a master stroke! We happy band of wine lovers would drink ourselves silly (at German expense), the wine consumed could fairly be claimed to have disappeared down British gullets, and upon arrival back in Blighty the finalists, nursing delicious hangovers, would rush home to friends, neighbours and work colleagues and say that German wine is hugely misunderstood, utterly delightfully easy to drink (and very freely available), and quite magnificent with food.

I first confronted the four finalists' beaming faces at Heathrow. I'd originally been asked to choose five but one had booked a holiday she couldn't cancel and so it was a quartet of thirsty tipplers, all women, which greeted me at Terminal Two. They were Jean Campbell, Angela MacMahon, Janice Walker and Julia Clarke. It caused comment when I first informed the organisers of the competition at the *Radio Times* that on the evidence of the written papers sent to me, which concerned themselves exclusively with commenting upon a new dry German wine called Kendermann Riesling 1995, that not a single man had made it through to the finals but the fact is the male entrants were not as accurate or as honest in their answers as the women. The men offered irrelevant and often flashy data in order to show off their knowledge and they never got close to the women's sensory response to and unpretentious analysis of the wine in the glass.

First night found us near the river Nahe making heroic efforts to reverse the ebb in the British consumption of German wine sales by swallowing as much local dry riesling as we could manage whilst eating all manner of Germanic tidbits. Our host was the charming and indefatigable Karl-Heinz Schmidt, the Kendermann company's export director, and the restaurant was owned and run by the Kruger-Rumpf vineyard and winery. Did I really eat hausgemachte Maultaschen auf Weinsauerkraut (gefult mit blut und Leberwurst)? My notes say so. I only remember Gargantuan-proportioned bulging squares like ravioli, truly homemade, filled with liver and blood sausage on a bed of sauerkraut fermented with wine. I ate with relish and downed glass after glass of the wine, wondering as each light dry deliciously flinty mouthful followed another, how superbly the gorgeous liquid went with the food. And the remarkable thing was I never felt stuffed. German wine is genuinely light and full of flavour and most examples do not rely upon alcohol for their impact. The Kruger-Rumpf wine was less than 10% (which compares with 12.5% to 13.5% with wines from other countries). The contestants' smiling faces as they ate variously of salmon and duck suggested they felt as I did. They were, even more than me, on a voyage of discovery.

The extent of the discoveries this short voyage would reveal made themselves apparent next day, the day of the final, where the four finalists were scheduled to examine and comment upon various German wines, the identities of which were concealed behind brown paper. Initially, the final paper merely asked candidates to guess the name of each wine, the grape, suggest its sweetness level and adduce various other technical aspects of it. However, I asked for an additional question to be put: what food would each wine ideally accompany? This is not an area the dyed-in-the-wool classic wine taster would consider essential information in order to arrive at an estimate of an individual's knowledge. But to me it is the bedrock of real wine nous and the basis of love of the liquid. For if you can successfully match a wine's flavour and texture with a particular dish, are you not thereby guiding that wine to its true destiny? The food it will most brilliantly accompany?

Wine is not made to be sniffed, swilled, gargled and spat, to end up in a spittoon in the chilly environment of a tasting room. It is meant to provide warmth in the dining room and finish as a delight and comfort to the digestion. To achieve success in the first location but to ignore the reality of the second is to misapply wine knowledge. I was pleased that the four finalists' efforts in this area were so striking. Julia Clarke, who eventually I adjudged to be the winner, was exemplary in this regard, apposite yet original, accurate but inspiring.

But of course the German wine producers, via their Deutsches Weininstitut, weren't just cheerfully putting on the finals, wining and dining us, and asking us to taste delicious wines because of four Englishwomen and my love of riesling. German wines need a boost and whilst, joking aside, it is encouraging to have the *Radio Times* organise wine competitions and for the likes of journalists like me to write about them, a somewhat more serious and strategically ambitious programme was, and is currently, in the process of taking place. It is nothing less than a revolution in German wine producing methods, nomenclature, bottling and labelling. And the day of the final, at the offices and production centre of Kendermann wines in the little town of Bingen upon Rhine, the full force, depth, and daring of this revolution struck me for the first time.

You know how German wines (when they're not made deliberately sweet) are so austerely dry, almost tart? This is because the so-called malolactic fermentation, which during or following the alcoholic fermentation, turns the sharp and appley malic acids to the soft and milky lactic acids, is inhibited. Australian whites, for example, all undergo this fermentation to a greater or lesser extent and it is this fruitiness, mellow and rich, which has influenced a whole generation of British wine drinkers. To our way of thinking, such bouncy buttery wines are the essence of fruitiness yet we consider them dry. To the Germans, such fruitiness is unthinkable. Until, that is, now. Until they saw what was happening to their sales in the UK. Thus, with the help of new world ideas and technology, certain major German wine producers are permitting the malolactic ferment to occur – to not much more than 20% in most cases if I'm any judge, whereas it can be anything from 40% to the whole hog in Australia. The German wines which have been permitted some malolactic fermentation taste different as a result. They taste fruitier but not what we would call sweeter.

The next step has been to make the names easier to swallow. Are you charmed, for example, to ask for Weisenheimer Mandelgarten Ortega Trockenbeerenauslese Rheinpfalz 1994? Now this is a very sweet dessert wine but who benefits from such a mouthful of a name, so typical of much of German wine names? The people who derive the most benefit are Germany's wine producing competitors who laugh themselves silly at the Komic Krauts' gothic nightmares on wine shelves. True, Blue Nun and Black Tower are old German favourites, and they're hardly impossible to get your tongue round, but the new German wines clunking off the bottling lines venture into areas no German wine producer would have dreamed of ten years ago. Devil's Rock Riesling is one such and it's almost now a veteran of the revolution. The '94 was a decent enough wine, once it got over its first nine months in bottle, the '95 was tasty too and the '96 had a touch of elegance. The '97 is advanced and interesting to drink.

Palatinarum Riesling and Palatinarum Rivaner are also new German bottling names and ideas. I can't say I'm crazy about the austerity of the riesling but the rivaner is delightfully whistle-clean. But the name? Palatinarum doesn't strike me as remotely enticing. The word surely suggests to the British mind not a region, which is its root, but an awkward shuffling-together of a place to keep fish (aquarium) and a building in which to view the heavens (planetarium). How about Fire Mountain Riesling and Black Soil Rivaner-Riesling? These are both made in the Pfalz region by Australian Linley Schultz and they have the added spice of being the product of a wine maker whose presence in a German winery, even as recently as five or six years ago, would have produced complete and utter incredulity. And what of some of the other adventurous, anglophonically named German wines streaming on to the market? Baden Dry, a standby for years, can now be found on the shelves in new guises – as Baden Pinot Blanc (a French grape name) and Baden Pinot Grigio (an Italian grape name). British names for some of the new wines include Amber Ridge, Silver Ridge, Slate Valley Dry Riesling, Slate Valley Country White, Wild Boar Riesling, North Star (Dry & Medium Dry), Villa Eden, 'K' Vineyards Riesling, Slate Valley, Four Rs, Northern Star, Lone Wolf, St Laurens, Solus (an excellent Thresher initiative) and, most adventurous of all with its strikingly shaped bottle in clear glass and novel label design, the wine referred to above, Bend in the River (so named for the famous bend in the Rhine – you Germans simply can't leave provenance and geography alone can you?).

And these wines are, I swear to you, are just the tip of the iceberg. The orchestra is only just warming up. The revolutionary concert hasn't really started yet. Even Blue Nun has done a little rejigging, though it hasn't abandoned the nun or its blueness.

I began my German trip thinking that it would be a fairly routine exercise where I could relax, drink some handsome wines and eat some terrific food (yet another aspect of German culture which is misunderstood and underrated). I simply thought that the wine competitors and I would be the ones who go delightfully mad on the Rhine. I finished the trip realising I'd got it completely the wrong nationality round. It's the Germans who have gone delightfully bonkers.

How is the revolution progressing? How are we drinkers appreciating the new German sense of humour? My own view is that the efforts to put new wine into new bottles can only be radically successful if it really is *new* wine. Permitting degrees of malolactic fermentation in riesling is not necessarily the answer; rivaner is a better grape variety to do it with and the results more becoming to British palates in the midst of a love affair with the lush, forward, fruitiness, perceived as dry, of the new world and, increasingly, the reformed regions of the old world like Apulia, Navarra, Conca de Barbera, Gascony, parts of the Languedoc and so on. I also don't much like some of the whacky names, labels and bottles but concede this is even more a matter of taste than grape variety. Personally, I wish it was with the more expensive, beautifully hand-crafted, single vineyard dry to off-dry rieslings of the Moselle, Nahe, the Pfalz, and the Rheingau that an education process was taking place because these are the truly great wines of Germany, most of them are massively undervalued at their humble prices (well under £10). Enjoyed at their peak of maturity, not too young, these wines are both stunning aperitifs as well as being forthright with many of the dishes we in the thick of the culinary multi-ethnicity of *fin-de-siècle* Britain now enjoy. They are also wonderful wines for the digestion and most examples are low in alcohol.

That these wines languish in popularity has not been given any reviving impetus by the rise in the popularity of new world fruit in the past ten years. German fruit is seen as either sickly sweet or tartly dry; whilst the beauty of new world wine is its poise and thrilling texture somewhere between the two. Just when, then, Germany might have found a fresh dynamic, along has come South Africa, Australia, Chile, New Zealand, California, plus the freshly activated regions of southern Europe (Spain, southern France and Italy particularly) which are turning out chardonnays in the new world mould.

Curiously, it is provenance which the new style German wines will find the greatest barrier to overcome. The drinker in the street simply doesn't *believe* the wines can be anything other than what they have always been perceived, rightly or wrongly, to have been. Maybe I'm wrong. Maybe I'm being too pessimistic. Maybe Bend in the River will galvanise a new generation of British drinkers into a radical reassessment of German wine.

But something tells me this won't happen. If I'm proved wrong, I'll happily sit down with Thresher's wine buying team, who were the first, I think, to put the wine on a retail shelf, and drink a bottle accompanied by my hat which I will ceremoniously eat.

With relish.

Health Warning!

Health Warning is an arresting phrase. I hope by employing it I may save you from working yourself up into a state. Let me explain.

I get a few letters a week from readers (both column and book) telling me that a wine which I have said is on sale in a certain store is not there and that the wine has either sold out or the branch claims to have no knowledge of it; I get letters telling me that a wine is a bit dearer than I said it was; and I get the odd note revealing that the vintage of the 16-point wine I have enthused about and which my correspondent desperately wants to buy is different from the one listed.

First of all, let me say that no wine guide in the short and inglorious history of the genre is more exhaustively researched, checked, and double-checked than this one. I do not list a wine if I do not have assurances from its retailer that it will be widely on sale when the guide is published. Where a wine is on restricted distribution, or stocks are short and vulnerable to the assault of determined readers (i.e. virtually all high rating, very cheap bottles), I will always clearly say so. However, large retailers use computer systems which cannot anticipate uncommon demand and which often miss the odd branch off the anticipated stocking list. I cannot check every branch myself (though I do nose around them when I can) and so a wine in this book may well, infuriatingly, be missing at the odd branch of its retailer and may not even be heard of by the branch simply because of inhuman error. Conversely, the same technology often tells a retailer's head office that a wine is out of stock when it has merely been completed cleared out of the warehouse. It may still be on sale on certain branches. Then there is the fact that not every wine I write about is stocked by every single branch of its listed stores. Every retailer has what are called retail plans and there maybe half-a-dozen of these and every wine is subject to a different stocking policy according to the dictates of these cold-hearted plans.

I accept a wine as being in healthy distribution if several hundred branches, all over the country not just in selected parts of it, stock the wine. Do not assume, however, that this means every single branch has the wine.

I cannot, equally, guarantee that every wine in this book will still be in the same price band as printed (these bands follow this introduction). The vast majority will be. But there will always be the odd bottle from a country suddenly subject to a vicious swing in currency rates, or subject to an unprecedented rise in production costs which the supermarket cannot or is not prepared to swallow, and so a few pennies will get added to the price. If it is pounds, then you have cause for legitimate grievance. Please write to me. But don't lose a night's sleep if a wine is twenty pence more than I said it is. If you must, write to the appropriate supermarket. The department and the address to write to is provided with each supermarket's entry.

Now the puzzle of differing vintages. When I list and rate a wine, I do so only for the vintage stated. Any other vintage is a different wine requiring a new rating. Where vintages do have little difference in fruit quality, and more than a single vintage is on sale, then I say this clearly. If two vintages are on sale, and vary in quality and/or style, then they will be separately rated. However, be aware of one thing.

Streetplonk sells a lot of copies. I say this not to brag but, importantly, to acquaint you with a reality which may cause you some irritation. When *Streetplonk* appears on sale there will be lots of eager drinkers aiming straight for the highest rating wines as soon as possible after the book is published. Thus the store wine buyer who assures me that she has masses of stock of Domaine Piddlewhatsit and the wine will withstand the most virulent of sieges may find her shelves emptying in a tenth of the time she banked on – not knowing, of course, how well I rate the wine it until the book goes on sale. It is entirely possible, therefore, that the vintage of a highly rated wine may sell out so quickly that new stocks of the follow-on vintage may be urgently brought on to shelf before I have tasted them. This can happen in some instances. I offer a bunch of perishable pansies, not a wreath of immortelles. I can do nothing about this fact of wine writing life, except to give up writing about wine.

Lastly, one thing more:

'Wine is a hostage to several fortunes (weather being even more uncertain and unpredictable than exchange rates) but the wine

*writer is hostage to just one: he cannot pour for his readers precisely
the same wine as he poured for himself.'*

This holds true for every wine in this book and every wine I
will write about in the years to come (for as long as my liver
holds out). I am sent wines to taste regularly and I attend wine
tastings all the time. If a wine is corked on these occasions,
that is to say in poor condition because it has been tainted
by the tree bark which is its seal, then it is not a problem
for a bottle in decent condition to be quickly supplied for me
to taste. This is not, alas, a luxury which can be extended to
my readers.

So if you find a wine not to your taste because it seems pretty
foul or 'off' in some way, then do not assume that my rating
system is up the creek; you may take it that the wine is faulty
and must be returned as soon as possible to its retailer. Every
retailer in this book is pledged to provide an instant refund for
any faulty wine returned – no questions asked. I am not asking
readers to share all my tastes in wine, or to agree completely
with every rating for every wine. But where a wine I have well
rated is obviously and patently foul then it is a duff bottle and
you should be compensated by getting a fresh bottle free or by
being given a refund.

How I Rate a Wine

Value for money is my single unwavering focus. I drink with my
readers' pockets in my mouth. I do not see the necessity of paying
a lot for a bottle of everyday drinking wine and only rarely do I
consider it worth paying a high price for, say, a wine for a special
occasion or because you want to experience what a so-called
'grand' wine may be like. There is more codswallop talked and
written about wine, especially the so-called 'grand' stuff, than
any subject except sex. The stench of this gobbledegook regularly
perfumes wine merchants' catalogues, spices the backs of bottles,
and rancidises the writings of those infatuated by or in the pay of

producers of a particular wine region. I do taste expensive wines regularly. I do not, regularly, find them worth the money. That said, there are some pricey bottles in these pages. They are here either because I wish to provide an accurate, but low, rating of its worth so that readers will be given pause for thought or because the wine is genuinely worth every penny. A wine of magnificent complexity, thrilling fruit, superb aroma, great depth and finesse is worth drinking. I would not expect it to be an inexpensive bottle. I will rate it highly. I wish all wines which commanded such high prices were so well deserving of an equally high rating. The thing is, of course, that many bottles of wine I taste do have finesse and depth but do not come attached to an absurdly high price tag. These are the bottles I prize most. As, I hope, you will.

20 Is outstanding and faultless is all departments: smell, taste and finish in the throat. Worth the price, even if you have to take out a second-mortgage.

19 A superb wine. Almost perfect and well worth the expense (if it is an expensive bottle).

18 An excellent wine but lacking that ineffable sublimity of richness and complexity to achieve the very highest rating. But superb drinking and thundering good value.

17 An exciting, well-made wine at an affordable price which offers real glimpses of multi-layered richness.

16 Very good wine indeed. Good enough for *any* dinner party. Not expensive but terrifically drinkable, satisfying and multi-dimensional – properly balanced.

15 For the money, a good mouthful with real style. Good flavour and fruit without costing a packet.

14 The top end of the everyday drinking wine. Well-made and to be seriously recommended at the price.

13 Good wine, true to its grape(s). Not great, but very drink-able.

12 Everyday drinking wine at a sensible price. Not exciting, but worthy.

11 Drinkable, but not a wine to dwell on. You don't wed a wine like this, though you might take it behind the bike shed with a bag of fish and chips.

10 Average wine (at a low price), yet still just about a passable mouthful. Also, wines which are terribly expensive and, though drinkable, cannot justify their high price.

9 Cheap plonk. Just about fit for parties in dustbin-sized dispensers.

8 On the rough side here.

7 Good for pickling onions or cleaning false teeth.

6 Hardly drinkable except on an icy night by a raging bonfire.

5 Wine with more defects than delights.

4 Not good at any price.

3 Barely drinkable.

2 Seriously – did this wine come from grapes?

1 The utter pits. The producer should be slung in prison.

The rating system above can be broken down into six broad sections.

Zero to 10   Avoid – unless entertaining stuffy wine writer.

10, 11   Nothing poisonous but, though drinkable, rather dull.

12,13   Above average, interestingly made. Solid rather then sensational.

14, 15, 16   This is the exceptional, hugely drinkable stuff, from the very good to the brilliant.

17, 18   Really wonderful wine worth anyone's money: complex, rich, exciting.

19, 20   A toweringly brilliant world-class wine of self-evident style and individuality.

Prices

It is impossible to guarantee the price of any wine in this guide. This is why instead of printing the shop price, each wine is given a price band. This attempts to eliminate the problem of printing the wrong price for a wine. This can occur for all the usual boring but understandable reasons: inflation, economic conditions overseas, the narrow margins on some supermarket wines making it difficult to maintain consistent prices and, of course, the existence of those freebooters at the Exchequer who are liable to inflate taxes which the supermarkets cannot help but pass on. But even price banding is not foolproof. A wine listed in the book at, say, a B band price might be on sale at a C band price. How? Because a wine close to but under, say, £3.50 in autumn when I tasted it might sneak across the border in winter. It happens, rarely enough not to concern me overmuch, but wine is an agricultural import, a sophisticated liquid food, and that makes it volatile where price is concerned. Frankly, I admire the way retailers have kept prices so stable for so many years. We drink cheaper (and healthier) wine now than we did thirty years ago. The price banding code assigned to each wine works as follows:

Price Band

A Under £2.50   B £2.50 to £3.50   C £3.50 to £5

D £5 to £7   E £7 to £10   F £10 to £13

G £13 to £20   H Over £20

All wines costing under £5 (i.e. A–C) have their price band set against a black background.

ACKNOWLEDGEMENTS

I owe this book to my family's indulgence and the back up of Linda Peskin. Sheila Crowley, Kate Lyall Grant, Katie Gunning, Jamie Hodder-Williams, Martin Neild, and Karen Geary at my dynamic publisher are also to be thanked. I am also grateful to Felicity Rubinstein and Sarah Lutyens, my delicious agents.

A few words on marriage.

Will Victoria Wine & Thresher find bliss?

The fat brewers don't understand wine. They mistrust it. It's something made by foreigners. The thin brewers, like the Londoner's Fullers with its chain of local wine shops, however, actually *drink* wine. The love affair of this nation with wine and the relegation of beer to a lesser division in drinkers' affections, forced the fat, conglomerated brewers to come to terms with the curious alien import. It was an uneasy relationship. Even in the case of Whitbread and Allied Domecq, who own Thresher and Victoria Wine respectively, there was a sense of a vinous cuckoo in the hop lover's nest. Will this change now that these two wine retailers, as announced in August this year, will settle down together and work out a meaningful relationship?

This announcement came just at the time when this book's introductions to these two retailers had already been set-up by the printer (I always get my introductions written several months before the wine rating sections are finalised). I am obliged, I feel, to comment on this situation since my introductions as they stand make no reference to it.

What difference will this union make to the reader, the user, of this wine guide? That is the most important question to me. And the answer is not much. Indeed, I suspect the merger will make little difference to the outward ethos of either operation this side of Christmas and so the wines listed under each retailer, and the fascias on the shops selling them, will not, in all likelihood, alter one jot. The Office of Fair Trading has yet to bless the merger at time of writing anyway, though no-one expects a hitch here.

Whether this not-before-time merger will effectively challenge the hegemony of the supermarkets, the reason for the merger's urgency, is open to doubt but we must express the hope that it will bring to the High Street a newly energised and competent set of wine shops which will offer the drinker somewhere genuinely outstanding to buy wine. (I do not by this refer to the wines themselves of which both sets of shops have admirable, if not perfect, ranges.) The slow, organic growth of Oddbins to a unique position is much admired by competitors (and, poorly, imitated), though claimed not to be profitable, and this expansion has matched the development in attitude, shop layout, staff knowledge and enthusiasm, followed by the dynamic recognition of the competitive rights of the consumer, which has taken place in other commercial enterprises (bookshops being among the best examples of these). There you have another impetus for the merger and for its owners, unable to find a buyer for either (which would have given each handy cash), to do the only thing to arrest the continual squeezing of margins which has often meant that achievable internal economies were achieved only by closing down less than successful branches.

Branch closure by each wine retailer over the past two years has been running at around 100 a year. This may well accelerate now (the combined number of branches is around 3000 – way too unwieldy). The new company, whatever it is called, will hardly be able to compete with itself if it can't compete with Tesco and Sainsbury on cost and Oddbins on image. Where, then, a Threshers wine shop is within lager bottle hurling distance of a VW off-licence, expect one or other to close, be sold off, and become a boutique or a hairdressing salon. The balance of closures will be heavier in some parts of the country than others. In Scotland, for example, where Thresher is weak, VW (with its Haddows shops), is strong. There is also the question of the plethora – though a kinder word might be merely abundance – of the so-called sub-brands within each wine shop set-up. Victoria Wine closes wine shops but opens more Wine Cellars. It also has Martha's Vineyard and the Firkin off-licence chain. Thresher has Wine Rack and Bottoms Up, Drinks Cabin and Huttons. Will they all get the boot? Will some names be kept? Some sort of sane rationalisation is patently necessary. To me, the number of various differently named branches each has been compelled to indulge in over the past decade since the supermarkets took such firm control of the wine market has smacked of retailing desperation. As if the attitude was 'we must do something, but we don't know precisely what it is, but anything is better than sitting on our backsides and doing nothing whilst the supermarkets slowly strangle us and so let's open some wine shops and call them . . . well, I rather like the sound of Drinks Cabernet . . . what do the rest of you chaps feel?'

Once the board of directors of the new set-up has sorted out premises (will it be Thresher's Welwyn or VW's Woking? Or pastures new?) and the new name, it will attend to rationalisation, redundancies, redeployment, and, this observer hopes, create a new wine retailing force altogether. The board – Jerry, Ralph, two Rogers, Bob, Brian, two Johns, and an Iain – has an average age of forty-six which does not suggest that this will happen quickly. It is a pity there are no women or wine-drinking ethnic minorities present on the board, though both exist in responsible positions at lower levels, and I suppose it would have been asking too much to have expected old-fogey-minded businesses like Whitbread and Allied to have hired as managing director a twenty-five year old ex-Oddbins branch manager and told her 'get on with it, matey, it's all yours.'

But, on second thoughts, is it asking too much? It is early days yet and nothing is outside the realms of possibility – not where the extraordinary British wine market is concerned.

FULLERS

BEER AND WINE DON'T MIX? DON'T TELL THAT TO ROGER HIGGS.

On the side of Fullers riverine brewery (for Fullers, let us not forget, brews Britain's greatest Thameside beer) is a protected tree which has, for some decades, crawled its way slowly but slowly up and across the old bricks. Since the appointment of Mr Roger Higgs as Fullers wine buyer (he came over from Oddbins a few years back) this tree is relishing a fresh lease of life and fruitfulness. Coincidence? Well, Fullers wine list has never been so inventively compiled nor have its London and Home Counties based wine shops been such lively places to acquire interesting wines.

That old tree has been an accurate metaphor for much of Fullers steady and stately progress over the years but the company's recent development into such things as 'The Fine Line', a female friendly chain of boozers offering Australasian cuisine and a list of worthy wines, confirms that the tree is blossoming anew* inspired by the exciting times the company is enjoying. The board's decision to borrow City money to expand its retail empire is impressive proof of this. Two 'The Fine Line' bars were opened in June this year, in SW10 and SW11, and further doors so I am told – in Canary Wharf, The Minories, Bow Churchyard, and Clapham – will have been opened by the time this book is published. I am now waiting for a friendly female to invite me out to dine in one (all invitations, please,

---

* I have absolutely no proof of this. It is sheer invention.

c/o The *Guardian* newspaper, EC1).

Quite what Alexander Pope*, once resident a few doors along from Fullers ancient tree, would have made of such establishments is difficult to guess. This guide can only drink to their continued expansion – not only on the grounds of style but also on the principle that if their wine lists succeed, and they are heavily slanted towards the new world, then this will feed through to the shops' shelves. Fullers confidence in its beers has been fully translated to its wines (none of which, of course, it makes itself) and this can only be good for the off-licence buyer of Fullers wines in the future. Mr Higgs' strengths in the new world are reflected in some terrific French wines and my belief is that the range will get tastier, broader, and more eclectic as time goes by.

The individual thirsty for an interesting experience can bring his or her appetite along to a Fullers shop in the ready expectation of being refreshed and satiated. As those appetites develop and expand, Fullers, it seems to me, has the means and increasingly the will to develop and expand along with it.

Fuller Smith & Turner plc
Griffin Brewery
Chiswick Lane South
London W4 2BQ
Tel: 0181 996 2000
Fax: 0181 995 0230

---

* Mr Pope wrote a great poem, 'An Essay on Criticism', on the subject of critics (which, in his purview at the time – 1711 – did not include critics of wine but nevertheless no wine writer could fail keenly to feel the sharp edge of the Papal intellect): ''Tis with our judgments as our watches, none/Go just alike, yet each believes his own.' 'A little learning is a dangerous thing;/Drink deep, or taste not the Pierian spring.' 'Good-Nature and good-sense must ever join;/To err is human, to forgive, divine.'

ARGENTINIAN WINE RED

Bonarda Tempranillo, J & F Lurton 1997

Lumpy little thing. A vulgar excrescence of nature.

Bright Bros Argentine Red, Mendoza 1997

Bit rough round the edge of the fruit but is this characterfulness?

Bright Brothers Argentine Tempranillo 1997 `15` `C`

Rather haughty in its own dry way. It's a delicious sipping wine, perhaps too dry for some, but the rich plum fruit is great with food.

Catena Malbec Lunluntu Vineyard 1995 `14.5` `E`

Juicy yet dry. Youthful yet mature. Sedate yet raunchy. Doesn't add up – but it does.

Gran Lurton Cabernet Sauvignon 1996 `15.5` `D`

Combines New World softness and forwardness with Old World tannins and stealth. Lovely food wine.

Isla Negra Reserve Syrah 1997 `16` `C`

Taint-free plastic cork leads to some wonderfully rich, deep, savoury fruit of dryness, decisiveness and daring deliciousness.

Isla Negra Syrah 1997 `16.5` `C`

Chocolate, raspberries, cherries, blackcurrants – no, no, stop: this wine is absurd enough without wrapping it in fruit – but one must add a touch of leather too. Altogether a superior glugging bottle. Has a wonderful bitter chocolate finish.

Malbec J & F Lurton 1997 `14.5` `C`

Tobacco scented, rich, very dry (almost brittle), and strong on the finish.

ARGENTINIAN WINE   WHITE

Alamos Ridge Chardonnay 1996 `15.5` `C`

It has such a nerve to cost this close to a fiver yet offer such wickedly classy fruit, creamy and textured and very very decisive that the average burgundy, asking four times more, is desolated.

La Rural Chardonnay 1997 `15` `C`

Has a fresh edge to some rich, melony fruit of class and precision.

AUSTRALIAN WINE   RED

Best's Great Western Dolcetto 1994 `15.5` `E`

Best's Victoria Shiraz 1996 `13` `D`

Tastes like a health tonic. Might be useful, made available on the National Health.

**Clancy's Shiraz/Cabernet Sauvignon/
Merlot/Cabernet Franc 1996** `15` `E`

Here the initial rich jamminess strikes as under adult but the character of finishing tannins gives it poise and maturity.

Four Sisters Shiraz Grenache, McLaren Vale 1996

Sisters without arms or, alas, much in the way of charms at six quid.

Grant Burge Old Vine Barossa Shiraz 1996

Medicinal, minty, polished, plummy, thickly textured, savoury, dry, gorgeous.

Hardys Bankside Shiraz 1996

Has some ruggedness to its essentially easy-going character.

Hardys Nottage Hill Cabernet Sauvignon/ Shiraz 1996

Elegant, rich, aromatic, balanced, most compellingly well priced, and more stylish than other vintages of the same brand.

Leasingham Grenache 1996

Ripeness but there are some rare tannins here, and nuttiness.

Lindemans Bin 45 Cabernet Sauvignon 1996

14 D

Juicy and jammy but the tannins buttress this softness and ripeness properly.

Lindemans Cawarra Dry Red 1997

13.5 C

Juicy Lucy.

Penfolds Rawsons Retreat Bin 35 Cabernet/Shiraz/Ruby Cabernet 1996

15.5 D

Rich, layered, clinging, ripe – a great steak and kidney pudding wine.

Peter Lehmann Barossa Grenache 1996 `14` `C`

Rosemount Estate Cabernet Sauvignon 1995 `14` `D`

Rosemount Shiraz 1996 `15.5` `D`

Not as soupy or as soppy as previous vintages. Here we have tannins and tenacity.

Rouge Homme Richardsons Red Block, Coonawarra 1994 `14` `E`

Shadrach Barossa Valley Cabernet 1993 `11` `G`

Yes, of course you'd accept a glass and murmur 'how nice'. But eighteen quid to buy! No way, Jose.

Stonewell Shiraz, Peter Lehmann 1992 `14` `G`

Astonishingly dry and deliberate. Bit wizened, but then it is ready to be buried beneath a side of roast beef.

AUSTRALIAN WINE   WHITE

Basedow Barossa Chardonnay 1995 `15.5` `E`

Grant Burge Late Picked Dry Muscat 1997 `15.5` `C`

Most unusual and very delicious. Sure, it's sweet(ish) but it has several layers to this elemental fruitiness and it has acidity. It's an original aperitif to serve to close friends.

Green Point Chardonnay 1996 `13.5` `E`

Far too expensive if not entirely malformed.

Hardys Nottage Hill Chardonnay 1997

Fantastic oily/buttery texture, ripe fruit, just terrific.

Ironstone Semillon/Chardonnay, Margaret River 1997

A rich, dry, crisp food wine of compelling double-faced furtiveness. It shows one side of itself which is soft and almost creamily fruity and then a crisp, raw delicious fresh face.

Jackdaw Ridge Semillon/Chardonnay 1996

Katnook Sauvignon, Coonawarra 1997

Its class tells in the end, and nine quid is a big end. The fruit is a touch squeamish of the acidity, which is only there to help, but with grilled scallops, say, this wine's disparate elements would gel wonderfully.

Madfish Bay Chardonnay 1997

Almost brash (but not quite), nearly dry (but deliciously not entirely), rich and eager (yet with a crisp, shy edge) – certainly it's in fine form.

Penfolds Rawsons Retreat Bin 21 Semillon/Chardonnay/Colombard 1997

The gorgeously rich '97 vintage strikes the palate with polish, purpose and plumpness.

Peter Lehmann The Barossa Semillon, 1997

Gorgeous display of two-faced insidiously delicious fruit. Has a soft, erotic ripe fruit on one hand and a rippling mineral acidity on the other.

Rosemount Estate Chardonnay 1996   `15.5` `D`

**Scotchmans Hill Chardonnay, Geelong
1995**   `11.5` `E`

Woody, vegetal, expensive.

CHILEAN WINE   RED

**Casa Lapostolle Cuvee Alexandre
Merlot 1996**   `17` `E`

One of Chile's great merlots thanks to its maker's utter mastery
of tannin and fruit and acid balance in the fruit not just in the
eventual wine. Wondrously textured, rich, ripe and classy.

Casa Lapostolle Merlot 1996   `15.5` `D`

Interesting French edge to soft, ripe fruit which gives the wine
some wry character and very rich food compatibility.

Casillero del Diablo Merlot 1996   `16` `C`

Has an edge of pesto and minestrone. But it's not all soup.
There's some tannin and acidity to give shape and recognisable
richness on the finish.

Cono Sur 20 Barrel Pinot Noir 1995   `14` `E`

Cono Sur Cabernet Sauvignon 1996   `15.5` `C`

Most approachable with its cherry/blackcurrant ferocity under-
cut by tannin and acid. Balanced, bonny, bouncy.

Cono Sur Pinot Noir 1997   `13` `C`

Cono Sur Pinot Noir Reserve 1996 `12.5` `D`

Errazuriz Merlot El Descauso Estate 1997 `16.5` `D`

So plump, ripe, purposeful and rich.

Errazuriz Reserve Syrah 1996 `18` `E`

Utterly magical fruit here of such sumptuous texture and temerity you almost hold your breath – defying nature as the wine descends the throat – hoping that the glorious richness won't lack anything as it finishes. It doesn't. It is world class all through.

Explorer Pinot Noir, Concha y Toro 1997 `15` `C`

Lovely vivid fruit which, curiously, finishes wickedly well textured yet angelically feral and warm.

La Palma Merlot 1997 `16` `C`

Elegant but very full and deep. Finishes dry but it starts with vigour and style.

La Palma Reserve Cabernet/Merlot 1996 `16` `C`

A real Chilean food wine: rich, dry, fully formed and throaty.

La Palma Reserve Merlot 1996 `14` `D`

With its smell of new leather you'd expect some richness from the fruit and this doesn't disappoint but it is very full and a touch sweet. It lacks any real tannin character or old world earthiness.

Mont Gras Ninquen Merlot 1996 `16` `E`

Huge richness and ripeness here, but also elegance and persistent excellence right through to the throat. Very rich texture, too.

Pupilla Luis Felipe Edwards Cabernet Sauvignon 1997

16.5 C

Captivating and haunting stuff. Has a lovely textured ripeness but the tone of the thing as it descends, and then lingers, is like Bach on the organ.

Valdivieso Malbec 1996

14 C

Getting a bit soft and pricey, isn't it?

Valdivieso Reserve Cabernet Franc 1996

16.5 E

Chinon meets Chateauneuf with a touch of Chianti. This bewildering internationalisation comes to us courtesy of the conjurors of Chile. What an alliterative masterpiece is to be found in this bottle!

Valdivieso Reserve Cabernet Sauvignon 1996

15 D

Vibrant richness, tonality and a good dry finish.

CHILEAN WINE WHITE

Casa Lapostolle Cuvee Alexandre Chardonnay 1996

17.5 E

It's the lingering stealth of the creamy, nutty finish (roast cobs on a bed of warm custard) which wins the day. It is sheer class and very individual. An exciting wine.

Concha y Toro Gewurztraminer 1997

13 C

A wine with a great future: its spiciness is subdued due to its youth. Lay it down to go with Thai food in AD2000+.

Errazuriz Reserve Chardonnay 1997 `16` `D`

Utterly hedonistic in its casual fruitiness, the forwardness of the richness is restrained by the acidity. It is not a gentle wine and it needs food.

La Palma Chardonnay 1997 `16` `C`

So winningly textured and warmly fruity for the money one is given cause for disbelief. A lovely, rich, classy, deep yet delicate mouthful.

Santa Ines Legado de Armida Chardonnay 1997 `17.5` `C`

It's the quality of the woody veneer which gives the wine such a polished finish and high-steppin', lithe, harmonious, richly fruity demeanour. Gorgeous stuff. Puts many a montrachet to shame.

Valdivieso Chardonnay 1997 `16.5` `C`

Amazing depth and vibrancy for such youth. Has plump fruit with a hint of tropicality and a rich, almost toffee edge to it. Utterly ravishing.

Valdivieso Reserve Chardonnay 1996 `14` `D`

Rich and textured if not hugely impactful on the finish.

FRENCH WINE RED

Chateau Beau-Site, St Estephe 1995 `15` `F`

Delicious biscuity texture and dryness. Very proper and adult if not quite X-certificate.

Chateau Belle-Garde Bordeaux 1995 `13.5` `D`

Chateau de Cazeneuve Grand Cuvee Pic St Loup 1996 `16.5` `D`

Violets, leather, earth, plum and blackcurrants – all wrapped up in a rich coating of warm tannicity.

Chateau de l'Euziere Cuvee des Escarboucles 1996 `16.5` `D`

Cheroots, dried leaves, old goat's cheese, mature shoe leather, compost – enough for you? It's delicious together. Try it.

Chateau de Lancyre Grand Cuvee Pic St Loup 1996 `16.5` `E`

Brilliant texture, polished yet characterful, with wonderful tannins attached to rich herby fruit. Superb performer with food.

Chateau du Trignon Sablet Cotes du Rhone Villages 1996 `15.5` `D`

Juicy, earthy, herby, textured, very ripe, full, opulent as it finishes. This is exceptional CdR.

Chateau Grand Renouil Canon, Fronsac 1994 `17` `F`

Very classy, classic claret with a touch of coffee. Great dry herbiness, big rich tannins, and that tobacco-edge to it all is just wonderful. A brilliant posh roast lamb dinner-party-with-candle-light wine.

Chateau Hautes Bages Monpelou, Pauillac 1995 `16.5` `E`

Very classy claret of stunning tannins, richness, and stylishly impactful finish.

Crozes Hermitage Petite Ruche, Chapoutier 1996

Bit juicy and simplistic.

DP2 Bourgogne Pinot Noir 1996

La Ciboise Cotes du Ventoux Chapoutier 1996

Juice with attitude. Soft and juicy yet bristly and vegetal.

Mas des Costes Pic St Loup 1995

16.5 D

Long dead cigars, fresh hillside herbs, dry warm earth, hedgerow fruits dying to drop – a fully alive wine is the result.

Valreas Domaine de la Grande Bellane, Cotes du Rhone Villages 1996 (organic)

13.5 D

Juice and very ripe. Touch of earth on the finish.

Wild Pig Reserve Shiraz 1996

Like a whacky Cotes du Rhone in mannerism and mode.

Winter Hill Red VdP de l'Aude 1997

Lovely polished richness and ripeness. Gorgeous plump texture and svelteness of fruit.

FRENCH WINE
WHITE

Bourgogne Chardonnay Ultra 35 1996

12 E

Chateau de Lancyre Pic St-Loup 1997 (rose)

14   C

Delicious richness yet pertness – so it's fresh, food friendly, and very quaffable.

Chateau Haut Grelot, Bordeaux 1997

14   C

I debated for a while before elevating it to 14. The price is at its peak for the level of fruit, but I decided to be kind to Bordeaux. A wine for shellfish.

Chateau Lacroix Merlot Rose 1997

13   C

Coteaux du Layon Chaume, Domaine de Forges 1996

15.5   E

Wonderful pineapple and pear-tinged honeyed fruit. Not brash and sweet, just bonny and serene. Great aperitif.

Fat Bastard Chardonnay VdP d'Oc 1997

15   D

Still fat, still a bastard, still worth keeping nine or twelve months before unloading the fruit (though it's drinkable now).

Le Pot Muscat Sec, Cotes Catalanes 1997

13   B

Doesn't quite grasp its spicy muscatiness fully enough, nor its crispness with sufficient grip.

Richemont Viognier 1996

15.5   C

A delicate, gently apricot and lemon wine which is excellent with smoked fish and will develop greater depth over the next year. Glorious alternative to chardonnay.

Sancerre Cuvee Flores, Vincent Pinard 1997

13   E

Bit like a clumsy Kiwi.

St Veran Deux Roches 1997

 16 D

Always one of Mr Higgs' classiest white burgundies, the '97 shows creaminess, ripeness, devious interplay between the fruit and the acidity, and a superb finish. 'France can win the world cup with whites like this,' I wrote before they did.

Virginie Sauvignon 1997

16 C

Wonderfully grassy but richly textured, gently nutty sauvignon of great class. Compelling price for such style, flavour and balance.

GERMAN WINE   WHITE

Serrig Herrenberg Riesling Kabinett, Bert Simon 1995

14 D

For riesling lovers, who can cellar their wines, this is a candidate for AD2005.

Weinheimer Sybillenstein Beerenauslese, Rheinhessen 1993, (half bottle)

 16.5 C

Superb, honeyed, nutty, sweet wine with rampant fruitiness and compatibility with fresh fruit and desserts, or just grapes and goat's cheese at the end of a meal.

ITALIAN WINE   RED

Avignonesi Rosso 1996

14.5 D

Blue plastic cork give the opportunity to show us untainted richness, earthiness and some degree of Chianti-like class.

Barocco Rosso del Salento 1997   13   B

Touch jammy.

Bragnolo Rosso VdT 1996   14   D

Interesting combination of juicy freshness and peppery wrinkliness.

Rustica Rosso di Sicilia 1997   13   B

Juicy yet, oddly, earthy.

Villa Pigna Colle Lungo Rosse delle Marche 1996   15.5   D

Delicious vivacious fruit of clarity and depth. Lovely fresh edge to the rich plums.

ITALIAN WINE   WHITE

Carato Chardonnay Barrique, Bidoli 1997   14   D

Classy nuts and stylish melons (with a hint of mineral acidity).

La Castagnola Chardonnay del Piemonte 1997   14   C

Warm, gently textured, bright on the finish. Some charm here.

Mezzo Mondo Chardonnay 1996   14   C

Very Italian in that it's difficult to conceive of its makers, putting this fresh, nutty wine together, that they weren't licking their lips and thinking of the food it would go with (shrimp risotto for one).

Rustica Bianco di Sicilia 1997 14.5 B

Plastic cork, witty label of high quality – do you need any other reason to touch this wine? Yes . . . it's made by a woman. (And it's clean, crisp and nutty.)

NEW ZEALAND WINE RED

Sacred Hill Basket Press Cabernet 1995 13 E

Juice! Who'll buy my squashed fruit?

NEW ZEALAND WINE WHITE

De Redcliffe Mangatawiri Chardonnay 1996 14 E

Interesting balance of fruit and acid. Not strident or woody or even hugely fruity, it's more one of those New World wines with one foot in the past.

Hunters Sauvignon, Marlborough 1997 14 E

Lot of money but the fruit here, finely cut and fresh, has some value.

Kim Crawford Marlborough Sauvignon 1997 14 D

Rather subtle, and perhaps expensive compared to similar and more exuberant (yet equally classy) expressions of the same grape now coming out of the Languedoc, Apulia and Chile. But it has texture and some subdued melon-edged fruit but it is of little value to food except the plainest and simplest grilled fish.

Kim Crawford Unoaked Chardonnay 1997 — 15.5 — D

Shows the great depth, untrammelled by wood, of pure Kiwi fruit. Gives Chablis a run for its money.

Montana Reserve Chardonnay 1997 — 14.5 — E

Classy, grassy, rich, confident, voluptuous.

Oyster Bay Marlborough Sauvignon Blanc 1997 — 16 — D

Most unusual and attention-grabbing. Has a delicate richness, almost smoky, a pineapple-tinged, mineralised freshness and a striking finish. A lovely fish wine.

Sacred Hill Barrel Ferment Chardonnay 1996 — 15.5 — E

Woody, chewy, busy, bright, soft yet with a hint of crispness, this is a very giving, rich wine of weight and wit.

Te Awa Farm Chardonnay, Hawkes Bay 1996 — 13.5 — E

Vavasour Single Vineyard Chardonnay 1996 — 10 — G

At least three and a half times more expensive than the fruit warrants.

PORTUGUESE WINE RED

Baga Bright Brothers 1995 `15.5` `C`

Aromatic, savoury, ripe, rich, dry to finish, this wine is game for almost anything: from duck breasts to pea and Parmesan risotto. It's excellently balanced, the elements chime perfectly together, and the finish is forceful yet agreeable.

Fiuza Cabernet Sauvignon 1995 `13.5` `C`

Quinto do Crasto Douro Tinto 1996 `14` `D`

Juicy but adult. Terrific with food.

PORTUGUESE WINE WHITE

Fiuza Sauvignon Blanc 1996 `13` `C`

SOUTH AFRICAN WINE RED

Bouchard Finlayson Galpins Pinot Noir 1996 `13` `E`

Lot of money for some decent aromatics.

Clos Malverne Pinotage 1997 `16.5` `D`

In the class of a Pic St Loup (qv any of Fullers' Fab Four) but with a wildness and unrestrained richness.

Fairview Zinfandel/Cinsault 1996 `16` `D`

Baked plums, vanilla, blackberries, a hint of creme caramel, and tannin. Now, is that a recipe for ambrosia or what?

Gwendolyn Shiraz/Cabernet Sauvignon 1996 `13` `E`

Jordan Cabernet Sauvignon 1995 `15.5` `E`

Creamed plums. What a stroke of fruity genius.

Kumala Reserve Cabernet 1997 `14` `E`

Black plastic is the cork. Black fruit is in the bottle.

Pinnacle Cabernet Shiraz 1996 `13.5` `D`

Savanha Cabernet Sauvignon 1997 `16` `D`

Brilliant vegetality and cabernet correctness. Solid and excitingly packed with fruit.

Savanha Shiraz 1997 `14` `D`

Lovely cigar scents here. The fruit is juicy and rich.

Scotchmans Hill Pinot Noir, Geelong 1995 `15` `E`

Better than loads of old tosh from the Cote d'Or. This wine is bold, smelly, ripe, truffley, rotting and farmyardy. Classic shit.

SOUTH AFRICAN WINE WHITE

Benguela Current Chardonnay 1997 `13` `C`

Bouchard Finlayson Oak Valley Sauvignon 1997　　12.5　E

Coast Line Chenin Blanc 1997　　12.5　B

Jacana Old Bush Vine Chenin Blanc 1996　　15.5　C

Jordan Barrel Fermented Chenin 1997　　13　D

Neil Ellis Chardonnay 1997　　15.5　E

Warm, elegant, nicely furnished with all the right fittings (acid, fruit in balance etc) but overall it's the confidence the wine exhibits which gives it its style.

Savanha Chardonnay 1997　　13　D

SPANISH WINE　　RED

Abadia Retuerta 1996　　15.5　F

Astonishingly svelte and polished. Fabulous texture.

Fuente del Ritmo Tempranillo La Mancha 1996　　15.5　C

Piles on the flavour with freshness and force. Great glugging here.

Marques de Grinon Dominio de Valdepusa Syrah 1995　　15.5　E

Such plumpness and richness – but only after the fruit has lingered for ten to fifteen seconds. This delayed action is the wine's charm.

Marques de Grinon Tempranillo 1996   15.5   C

A gentle wine with a bit of a rich wallop in its finish. Not a powerful wine but an impactful one.

Vina Albali Gran Reserva 1989   15.5   D

Front label like a travel brochure encourages the fruit to go all over the place. Superb maturity, raisiny richness: plums, blackcurrants, almonds and a hint of anise and vanilla.

SPANISH WINE   WHITE

La Vega Verdejo/Sauvignon 1997   14.5   C

Has an acquired taste of sourness and herbaceousness. Might be splendid with oysters Rockefeller.

USA WINE   RED

Fetzer Bonterra Cabernet 1995 (organic)   15   E

Rich, rounded, full, Californian in ripeness and tannic cosiness from nose to throat.

Fetzer Syrah 1996   16   E

Gives syrah a new dimension of tannic spiciness. Wonderful richness and ripeness here.

Saintsbury Garnet Pinot Noir 1996   13   E

Rich and smelly (farmyardy and wild raspberryish) but fails to finish on a tenner's worth of value.

Schug North Coast Pinot Noir 1995 `12` `E`

Thornhill Barbera NV `14.5` `C`

Thornhill Pinot Noir NV `13` `C`
Good stab.

USA WINE
WHITE

Bonterra Viognier 1996 (organic) `15` `E`

Curious delayed action spiciness here. There is a delicious delicacy to it which rich food will ruin, so it's best kept for grilled fish and chicken (breast of, with a cream sauce).

Fetzer Bonterra Chardonnay 1996 `14.5` `E`

Fetzer Sundial Chardonnay 1996 `14.5` `D`

Impressive finesse yet fullness here. Rich and warm yet crisp and beautifully balanced. Has great elegance.

Fetzer Vineyards Dry Gewurztraminer, Mendocino 1997 `15.5` `D`

Really dry, gently spicy and fruity without being remotely sweet. An individual specimen of some class.

Redwood Trail Chardonnay 1995 `15.5` `D`

Seems to aim for a boisterousness which, thankfully, it doesn't quite achieve. Settles down richly in the throat, rather deliciously.

Thornhill Chardonnay NV `15.5` `C`

FORTIFIED WINE

**Stanton & Killeen Liqueur Muscat
(half bottle)** `15` `D`

Wonderful with a creme brulee, ice cream or a slice of Christmas pud.

SPARKLING WINE/CHAMPAGNE

Champagne Brossault Brut NV `13` `F`

Appley and fresh.

Champagne Brossault Brut Rose `13` `F`

Chateau de Boursault Champagne Brut `13.5` `G`

Joseph Perrier Champagne NV `12.5` `G`

**Moet's Shadow Creek Blanc de Noirs
(USA)** `14` `E`

Pelorus 1993 (New Zealand) `15.5` `G`

Yeasty, rich, classy and very stylish on the finish.

Seaview Pinot Noir/Chardonnay 1994 (Australia)

 16 E

One of Australia's strongest and tastiest challenges to Rheims' hegemony.

Veuve Clicquot Rich Reserve 1989

13 H

Has some class – at £34 it ought to, but is it worth it? Not quite.

MAJESTIC

MASON EXPANDS HIS EMPIRE! A MILLIONAIRE SHARE-HOLDING EMPLOYEE IN EVERY BRANCH?

The timetable tells its own story:

June 1997 – Majestic announces a 60% rise in pre-tax profits to £1.98 million following its flotation in November on the Alternative Investment Market.

August 1997 – Majestic opens its first store in Scotland in Glasgow.

September 1997 – Majestic reports operating profits of £939,000 for the half year to end of September, double the same period last year. Turnover was up by 21% to £26.5 million – seems to have impressed the City since the flotation in November 1996.

September 1997 – Majestic wins Off Licence Retailer of the Year Award in the annual Reed Retail Awards.

February 1998 – Majestic announces major store opening programme. It plans to open 10 new stores a year for the foreseeable future. It believes there is room to double in size. In February 1998, the retailer had 70 stores.

July 1998. Majestic's sales over their financial year ending March are preliminarily reckoned to be up to over £60-million. That means sales are up 21% on the previous year.

The above set of figures does not really get beneath the skin of what Majestic is about. Majestic is unique. It is the only wine retailer about whom I write which has the nous, the financial clout, and the wit to buy wine like commodities used to be bought in the old days when there were colonies to exploit. For far-flung exotic outposts, then, read Sweden. The decision by the State Liquor Board of that country to flog off much of its stock, especially mature claret, has been an opportunity which Mr Tony Mason, the man who inspires Majestic's wine buying operations, was unable to resist. The result has been some superb reds, at the peak of their drinkability, at prices to make the drinker rub his eyes in disbelief. Majestic really loves its wine (not all wine retailers love it as much).

Majestic's customers spend money. Their average spend on a bottle is nearer a fiver than the supermarkets' £3. This means many customers spend nearer double that average; those who felt confident enough to cough up seven, eight or nine quid on certain of those Swedish clarets got a bargain.

It is that sort of customer relationship which is priceless. Majestic believes there is room for it to double in size? I'd say quadruple. The only question is this: which wine shop chain would it be rational to buy, raising the money through share splits and an investment bank, in order to achieve this expansion?

You may say but surely Majestic is a wine warehouse concept. How can it develop wine shop sites? My response to that is that if the wine shops (like Victoria Wine and Oddbins) can move into warehousing, why can't Majestic cross into their territory?

Something to think about, Mr Mason.

Majestic Wine Warehouses
Odhams Trading Estate
St Albans Road
Watford WD2 5RE
Tel: 01923 816999
Fax: 01923 819105

SEE STOP PRESS SECTION AT END OF BOOK FOR LAST-MINUTE ADDITIONS OR UPDATES TO THIS RETAILER'S RANGE.

ARGENTINIAN WINE   RED

Correas Syrah, Mendoza 1996   `14.5` `C`

A rich, dry, fruity wine with a hint of vegetality plus warmth
to it which give it food compatibility and sipping style.

Correas Syrah Sangiovese, Mendoza 1996   `16` `C`

Great earthy richness, concentration, tannic maturity and a
lingering finish of spiced plum and blackcurrant.

Marques de Grinon Diminio de Agrelo
Malbec 1996   `16` `D`

A very stylish malbec. Has perfume, presence, persistence, loads
of flavour, dryness and depth, and a finish of considerable finesse
yet weight.

Marques de Grinon Tempranillo, Mendoza
1996   `16` `C`

Will soften over the next two years but eminently drinkable
now – the rich tannins strike with potency but the fruit's all
there, rich and deep, and good robust food will bring it out
beautifully.

AUSTRALIAN WINE   RED

Angove's Classic Reserve Cabernet
Sauvignon 1996   `14` `C`

Juicy quaffability. Rich and ready.

Angove's Classic Reserve Shiraz 1996 15 C

Simply, it's Australia at the right price with the right soupy dryness and sunny, rich characterfulness. Sensuous, ripe, fun, this is what it's all about: sheer textured pleasure.

Cape Mentelle Cabernet Merlot 1995 16.5 E

Such classy tannins and complexity of fruit (blackcurrant being the predominant theme) that it is a lesson in assembly, fruit quality and, best of all, that pizzazz, that rich savoury punch on the finish.

Ironstone Shiraz Grenache, Margaret River and Swan Valley 1996 16.5 D

Takes shiraz into a new dimension of such balance of fruit, acid and tannin, all so deftly interwoven and gorgeously textured, that it makes offerings from other Oz regions seem either mean or too expensive. It's a terrific wine with a hint of wildness.

James Halliday Cabernet Sauvignon, Coonawarra 1994 13 E

Juicy.

Lindemans Bin 45 Cabernet Sauvignon 1996 14 D

Juicy and jammy but the tannins buttress this softness and ripeness properly.

Mamre Brook Cabernet Shiraz 1994 13 D

Juicy.

Misty Mooring Shiraz 1997

Light, and pleasantly quaffable.

**Penfolds Rawson's Retreat Bin 35
Cabernet/Shiraz/Ruby Cabernet 1996**

Rich, layered, clinging, ripe – a great steak and kidney pudding wine.

AUSTRALIAN WINE WHITE

**Angove's Classic Reserve Chardonnay
1997**

Great under-a-fiver value here: rich, crisp, dry, expansive yet stylish.

**Cape Mentelle Semillon/Sauvignon
Blanc 1997**

Yes, it's expensive but it is very classy. The grip of the wine is considerable, rare in a dry white, and the gently melony fruit also hints at a very subtle leafiness.

**Ironstone Semillon/Chardonnay, Margaret
River 1997**

A rich, dry, crisp food wine of compelling double-faced furtiveness. It shows one side of itself which is soft and almost creamily fruity and then a crisp, raw delicious fresh face.

Ironstone Vineyards Gold Canyon Chardonnay 1996

Curiously haughty richness to the dryness – bit stiff-upper-lippish. Odd in an Australian but not unattractive.

Lindemans Bin 65 Chardonnay 1997

The '97 vintage! Under a fiver! Rich, silky, aromatic, clean fruit. Terrific stuff . . .

Mountadam Chardonnay, Eden Valley 1995

16 F

Wonderful oily texture with a subtle, very subtle, hint of peat on the aroma and on the gorgeously rich finish. This elegant, alcoholic earthiness makes the wine a complex beast of huge charm. I wish it were cheaper.

Penfolds Rawsons Retreat Bin 21 Semillon/Chardonnay/Colombard 1997

15 C

Seemingly casually attired at first meeting, it reveals some jazzy habiliments as it progresses from nose to throat.

Preece Chardonnay, Michelton 1996

Packed with ripe fruit from apricots to spiced pineapple and pear. But, for all that, it's not oppressive or overblown. It achieves a measure of hugely quaffable elegance.

Wynns Coonawarra Riesling 1997

Has real riesling class, texture and mineral impact.

Yalumba Barossa Reserve Verdelho 1996

15 E

Toasty and food friendly. Be great with lightly spicy oriental fish dishes.

CHILEAN WINE RED

Carta Vieja Antigua Cabernet Sauvignon 1996

It pulls off that delicious two-card trick at which Chile excels. It offers juicy ripeness with superbly tasty tannins. Smashing glugging here.

Carta Vieja Merlot 1997

Very chewy and full of flavour. Big, rich, textured fruit. Finishes dry.

Luis Felipe Edwards Carmenere 1997

Chocolate, coffee and dry cassis. A hugely rich wine, but with backbone, thanks to the tannins and concentrated richness of finish.

Luis Felipe Edwards Reserva Cabernet Sauvignon 1996

A cabernet lover's dream: tannic pertness, rich vegetal fruit with hints of green pepper and white pepper, balance, tenacity on the palate, and huge drinkability. One of the most classic Bordeaux style of Chilean cabs, it provides a smooth yet eventful ride.

Pupilla Luis Felipe Edwards Cabernet Sauvignon 1997

Captivating and haunting stuff. Has a lovely textured ripeness but the tone of the thing as it descends, and then lingers, is like Bach on the organ.

Santa Rita Reserva Cabernet Sauvignon, Maipo 1996

Hints of the cigar box Uncle Egbert's had since 1914, but the finish of the fat fruit is not so battle-scarred – it's all rich, soft fruit of great depth and savour.

CHILEAN WINE   WHITE

Luis Felipe Edwards Chardonnay 1997

Big richness of tone, gently creamy and deep, with a lovely underlying nuttiness.

FRENCH WINE   RED

Beaune Clos des Avaux 1er Cru, Baptiste Brunet 1995

No, it won't do at twelve quid. It barely does at five.

Bourgogne Pinot Noir Delauney 1996

Bourgogne Rouge, Leroy 1996

Some texture and classy tannins but twelve quid?

Bouton d'Or Cairanne, Cotes du Rhone Villages 1995

Dry, herby, brambly fruited, good balance and fine finish. A touch of elegance underscores the richness of the fruit. Brilliant value for food or mood.

Cabernet Franc Domaine de l'Ile St-Pierre 1996

15.5 B

Superb dry wild raspberry fruit with a hint of freshly sharpened pencil (HB, I fancy) and this makes it typical cab franc but not typically priced. A grand glug for the dry palated. Great with food.

Chateau Coufran, Haut Medoc 1992 (half bottle)

15 B

Chateau Coufran, Haut Medoc 1993 (half bottle)

13.5 C

Chateau de Flauguergues Coteaux du Languedoc 1996

17 D

Beautiful violet-scented fruit of depth, flavour, power, great class and consummate balance of elements: fruit/acid/tannin. An impressive bigness without towering imbalance or over-done-ness.

Chateau de Lisse, St Emilion 1993 (half bottle)

14 C

Chateau de Luc Corbieres 1996

15.5 C

Aromatic, ripe, rich, warm, vivid, concentrated, herby and full of hedgerow fruitiness. A deeply engaging wine of character and class.

Chateau la Perriere, Bordeaux 1996

13 C

Curious dryness then juicy ripeness as it finishes.

Chateau Ludon-Pomies-Agassac, Haut-Medoc 1995

13 F

Youthful, needs time to develop its attack.

Chateau Roumanieres, Coteaux du Languedoc 1996

14 | C

Curious clash of ripeness and earthy dryness which only food can resolve.

Chateau St James Corbieres 1994

14 | C

Has some really attractive gamey qualities. Match with a grouse perhaps?

Chateauneuf-du-Pape, Domaine des Senechaux 1996

14 | E

Almost loses its grip but wins in the end. Gorgeous fruit and texture.

Chinon les Garous, Couly-Dutheil 1997

15 | D

Gorgeously blackcurranty and raspberryish with astonishingly well developed fruit of great polish and wit. Considering its youth this is a well advanced cab franc.

Chiroubles Domaines Desmures, Duboeuf 1997

11 | D

Claret Lot 278, Bordeaux 1997

15 | C

Terrific claret! Real hints of real classic stuff but in an eminently quaffable style.

Coteaux de Tricastin Domaine Saint Remy 1997

15.5 | C

Brilliant little wine of substance and style. Lovely ripe, deeply polished texture with a delicious plumpness and purpose. A very low-class of price tag for such a high class of fruit.

Coteaux de Tricastin Domaine Vergobbi 1994
`17` `C`

Astounding richness, depth, sturdiness, weight and pure hedonistic delight. It puts to shame many a Chateauneuf-du-Pape at three times the price. Coffee, tobacco, plum, nuts, raisins, blackcurrants – I could go on through the whole tobacconist, past the fruiterers, and end up in . . . in an old club armchair.

Cotes du Rhone Les Chevaliers au Lys d'Or 1997
`14` `B`

Convincingly soft, unearthy, ripe and very drinkable. Has some character in spite of being so soft and ripe.

Domaine Bois du Garn Grenache Syrah, Cotes du Vivarais 1996
`15.5` `C`

Molar-gripping bargain. Earthy, ripe, rich, nicely modern yet with an old fashioned finish.

Domaine de la Janasse VdP de la Principaute d'Orange 1996
`16.5` `D`

Lovely earthy edge to some plump, fulfilling fruit of richly textured, ripe fruitiness with beautifully evolved tannins. Terrific.

Domaine des Murettes, Minervois 1995
`16` `C`

Delicious fruit here with a dry, herby, sun-warmed edge and a palate-soothing softness and wry richness. Country wine, yes, but with a touch of class.

Fixin Jaffelin 1995
`11` `E`

Grenache/Cabernet VdP de l'Ardeche 1997
`16` `B`

What magnificent value here! Has hints of the peppery cabernet to match the juiciness of the grenache and the result is an excitingly underpriced plonk of rare quaffability and style.

Hautes Cotes de Beaune La Daligniere 1995

`12.5` `D`

Hentall's Syrah Les Ocres, VdP d'Aigues 1997

`14` `C`

Soft, rounded, fat, full – but very satisfying. Give it a good shake to dissipate the sulphur upon opening.

La Cuvee Mythique Vin de Pays d'Oc 1995

`13.5` `D`

Not in the class of the '94. It's not a poor wine, simply well in excess, money-wise, of the fruit on offer.

Mas des Bressades Cabernet Syrah VdP du Gard 1995

`16.5` `D`

Superb rustic elegance! A sunny, deeply dry yet richly, rollingly fruity wine of brilliant tannins and characterful stylishness. Makes a mockery of many a Bordeaux at three times the price.

Morey St Denis, Baptiste Brunet 1995

`10` `F`

Fearful price for fearful fruit.

Morgon Jean Descombes 1997

`12.5` `D`

Pernand-Vergelesses, Jaffelin 1995

`11` `E`

Pinot Noir Cave de Ribeauville 1996

`16` `C`

Superb wild raspberry and cherry fruit with a hint of the farmyard, to remind us it's pinot, and it has the elemental pinot quality that Kiwis, for example, would give their eye teeth for: a tightly defined fruit with a hint of bonny rot. Well, it's all rot anyway, wine writing, don't you think?

Regnie Domaine Vallieres 1997 `15` `C`

The most drinkable, characterful, dryly wry Beaujolais I've tasted for some while, under a fiver.

St Joseph, Bernard Gripa 1995 `12.5` `E`

Wild Pig Red VdP d'Oc 1997 `16` `B`

Brilliant glugging value! Soft, ripe, it assuages the day's devilments and drearinesses. Has the plummy pertness to accompany chillied tomato soup (*my* recipe!).

FRENCH WINE   WHITE

Big Frank's Viognier VdP d'Oc 1997 `15.5` `C`

Lovely ripe plumpness of texture, apricot-fresh and deep. Yet it's dry, shows great faithfulness to the wishes of the grape, and it finishes well.

Bourgogne Blanc, Leroy 1996 `10` `F`

I simply find it impossible to reconcile a £12 price tag with this level of fruit.

Bourgogne Chardonnay Meilleurs Climats, Emile Trapet 1997 `14` `C`

Decent, minor white burgundian. Well, how often do these things gel under a fiver? Great nuttiness of approach to the fruit.

Cante Cigale Rose de Saignee, VdP de l'Herault 1997

`14` `C`

Character here! Rare in a rose!

Chablis, Caves les Viticulteurs de Chablis 1996

`15.5` `D`

An excellent, crisp, rich-edged Chablis of charm and precision. Terrific price for such style – a rare Chablis.

Chablis Domaine Vocoret 1997

`12` `E`

Chalonnaise Chardonnay, Cave de Buxy 1996

`13.5` `C`

With food it's a solid proposition (even a spicy grilled chicken wing) but it lacks real definition as a quaffing bottle.

Chardonnay Cuvee Australienne, VdP du Jardin de la France 1997

`13.5` `C`

Chardonnay Jean de Balmont, VdP du Jardin de la France 1997

`14` `B`

Some forthrightness and unfussily charming fruit here.

Chardonnay Vin de Pays d'Oc, Ryman 1995

`16` `C`

One of the Pays d'Oc's tastiest and most stylish chardonnays under a fiver. The richness is controlled, balanced and in perfect harmony with the acidity – thus the overall texture is high class.

Chateau de Sours Rose 1997

`13.5` `D`

Elegant but pricey.

Chateau Haut Mazieres Blanc, Bordeaux 1996

`15.5` `C`

Delightfully dry and food friendly. It has a somewhat chewy edge, crisp and decisive, and the fruit is relaxed yet firm. An elegant under-a-fiver Bordeaux blanc.

Chateau la Jaubertie Blanc, Bergerac 1997

`16` `C`

A deliciously grassy sauvignon, perhaps the most accomplished in the new world style in France. It hints at richness but this restraint is all part of its charm.

Chateau Meaume Bordeaux Rose 1997

`14.5` `C`

Elegant and amusingly hoity-toity.

Chenin Blanc VdP du Jardin de la France, Remy Pannier NV

`14.5` `B`

Crisp, clean, fresh, hints of mineralised fruit. At £2.99, you can't buy much more.

Gewurztraminer Materne, Haegelin 1997

`16` `D`

Unusually New World-ish gewurz in its richness, fatness, spicy butteriness and fullness.

Gewurztraminer Vendanges Tardives Furstentum, Bott-Geyl 1994 (50cl)

`15` `G`

Lovely spicy, honeyed fruit, rich and textured, and it's a great wine for fresh fruit.

Grand Ardeche Chardonnay, Louis Latour 1996

`13.5` `D`

Some flavour and richness here. Seven quids' worth? Not quite.

Hentall's Les Ocres Clairette, VdP de Vaucluse 1997

16 C

One of the plumpest and crispest whites you can buy. Delicious richness, fullness yet without blowsiness or straining too hard for effect.

Les Grand Clochers Chardonnay, VdP d'Oc 1997

14 D

New World in thrust, Old World in balance. Rich and flavoursome.

Marc Bredif Vouvray 1995

15 E

Wet wool, ripe melon, green plums – it is too young to be at its best. Can you wait five or six years? Or even longer if you want this dry Vouvray to show us its true vivacity and depth.

Montagny 1er Cru, Chateau du Cray 1996

14 D

A deliciously clean, limpid Montagny with very little overblown woodiness – as is sometimes the case. Has some fresh, clean elegance.

Montlouis Clos de Cray 1995

16 D

An immensely interesting and ambitious wine which is rather numb-er than it will be in eight to ten years when it will blossom more excitingly. Still, try a bottle now, whilst it's in nappies, to get the feel of the minerals and dry honey.

Moulin Touchais, Coteaux du Layon 1986

16.5 E

Gorgeous toasted honey fruit with nuts and sesame seeds.

Muscadet sur Lie Chateau de Goulaine 1996

13.5 C

Getting better. Must try harder next term.

Muscadet sur Lie Grand Mouton, Louis Metaireau 1996

| 11 | D |

Touch unrealistic.

Muscat de Rivesaltes, Chapoutier 1996 (half bottle)

| 15.5 | C |

A delicate, honeyed wine with a hint of satsuma and pineapple – just hints. Perhaps it's too delicate for rich puds. With fresh fruit after a feast, it's a feast in itself.

Pinot Blanc Haegelin d'Alsace 1996

| 14 | C |

Personally, I'd lay this wine for two more years yet. It'll be richer and spicier.

Pouilly Vinzelles Chateau de Laye 1997

| 15 | E |

One of the cutest examples of the breed I've tasted in years. Has real character, yet bite and freshness.

Reuilly, Beurdin 1997

| 13.5 | D |

A touch austere but far from unexciting. The price makes it a buy for the buff (who is into regional French quirks) but the rest of us may say 'where's the rest of the fruit?'

Riesling Bollenberg, Haegelin 1996

| 13 | D |

Riesling Grafenreben, Bott-Geyl 1996

| 14 | E |

I'd be inclined to cellar it four or five more years yet. It has a promising future.

Sancerre 'Clos du Roy', Paul Millerioux 1996

| 13 | D |

Sauternes Rothschild 1994 (half bottle)   `10` `D`

Sauvignon de Touraine, Domaine Joel Delaunay 1997   `14.5` `C`

Has some genuine regionality in its hint of earth and minerals. Excellent wine for all things oceanic (seaweed excepted).

Sauvignon Lot 279, Bordeaux 1997   `13.5` `C`

I'd love to rate it higher but it doesn't help itself on the finish. Pity. It has something going for it.

Tokay Pinot Gris Ribeauville 1997   `15.5` `D`

Terrific chewy dried apricot fruit here with a tendency to nerves. I love TPG when it's in this sort of mood. A quaffing wine.

Tokay/Pinot Gris, Haegelin d'Alsace 1997   `16` `D`

A spicy, peachy, soft yet dry, creamily-edged TPG with loads of flavour and depth. A wine for oriental food.

Vin de Pays de Vaucluse, Pellew 1996   `15.5` `B`

Quite brilliant value. A crisp nutty wine which dares to hint at a minor white burgundy. Snap it up!

Vouvray Demi-sec, Domaine Bourillon Dorleans 1997   `15` `D`

Superbly raw youth (though has puppy fat). It'll age for five to seven years and worth laying down at this price. It will reveal beautiful dry honey character as it ages.

Vouvray Tris de Nobles Grain, Domaine Bourillon Dorleans 1995 (50cl)   `16` `F`

Beautiful richness and ripeness. Put it down for a few years and it'll be even more complex.

GERMAN WINE

Bechtolsheimer Sonnenberg Ortega Trockenbeerenauslese 1994 (37.5cl)

Has a lovely, chewy finish to complement the strident honey richness.

Dirmsteiner Schwarzerde Beerenauslese, Sichel 1994 (37.5cl)

Huge richness, swimming in fruit and acidity and it is powerfully sweet and rich in the finish. Will age for ten to fifteen years.

Grans Fassian Trittenheimer Altarcher Riesling Kabinett 1996

2010 AD? Yep, I really think so. It needs time.

Grans Fassians Riesling, Mosel 1997

Somewhat young and muted and a bit confused to find itself out in the world. Best not opened for at least six or seven years.

Jean Baptiste Kabinett, Weingut Gunderloch 1996

Complex, young, precociously well-developed, nutty, subtly minerally-edged, this is an extremely elegant, highly sophisticated specimen of huge charm. A wonderful aperitif.

Nackenheimer Rothenberg Riesling Spatlese, Weingut Gunderloch 1996

Needs five or six years to achieve its destiny (16/17 points possibly).

Oberemmeler Rosenberg Riesling Kabinett Halbtrocken 1993

`14` `C`

Needs five years to flesh out the bones but it's still a lovely aperitif tipple: fresh, cutting, old-fashioned, witty.

Ruppertsberger Hofstuck Riesling Kabinett, Winzerverein 1995

`13.5` `C`

Serriger Heiligenborn Riesling Spatlese 1990

`15.5` `C`

Mineral richness, ripeness and depth give the wine simplicity and precision. A captivating aperitif of uniquely Germanic charms.

ITALIAN WINE
RED

Amarone della Valpolicella, Tedeschi 1993

`14` `E`

Figgy, raisiny, yet dry – not as exuberant or as dizzily cherry rich as some but a fine food wine.

Barbera d'Asti, Prunotto 1996

`14` `D`

Amusing quaffing wine with ripe cherry as its theme, coated in a brisk earthiness.

Barone Cornacchia Montepulciano d'Abruzzo 1996

`14` `C`

Jammy, dry, rich, fresh, characterful, brilliant with food.

Basilicata Rosso 1996

`15.5` `B`

Thundering good value from the volcanic soil of this curious region, this wine is highly drinkable, fresh, gently individual without being too hairy or scary.

Capitel Ripasso San Rocco, Tedeschi 1993

This is the essence of Veronese simplicity and elegance. Gorgeously rich, gently figgy with a hint of cherry bitterness but it's so lushly drinkable and food friendly. It's also, incredibly, dry to finish.

Cavalchina Bardolino 1997

Light and cherryish, but very cheering and Italian, in that it is wonderfully with-shellfish quaffable. A risotto wine – even.

Centine Saint'Antimo, Banfi 1996

Cortenova Merlot, Grave del Friuli, Pasqua 1997

Dogajolo, Toscano Carpineto 1996

Interesting and very individual Tuscan red with a dry, leafy fruit as striking as its autumnal label.

Nipozzano Riserva Chianti Rufina Frescobaldi 1995 16 E

The wines of this estate always seem to tread that gorgeous line between meaty chewiness and earthy richness, and lithe fruitfulness of an inexpressibly youthful demeanour. Elegance is the thought here, I suppose.

Recioto della Valpolicella, Tedeschi 1991 (half bottle) 13 D

Needs a few hours to develop after opening the bottle. Good with a veg and fruit curry.

Remole Chianti Frescobaldi 1996 `15.5` `D`

Very rich, dark cherry fruited, savoury-to-finish Chianti, not remotely earthy. Considerably friendlier than many, it is very deep and savoury.

Valpolicella Classico, Santepietre 1997 `10` `C`

Very juicy.

ITALIAN WINE WHITE

Castello di Tassarolo, Gavi 1996 `15` `D`

The so-called 'great' white of Piedmont, made in the Gavi area, from the cortese grape and this is, by reputation, one of its wittiest exponents. It smells woolly, creamy, nutty and has a crisp yet overripe finish. Beguiling!

Cavalchina Bianco di Custoza 1997 `16` `C`

A custardy Custoza! What a lovely tipple. Not blowsy or too creamy, no; the crisp appleskin acidity melds perfectly with the richer overtones to provide class, style and drinkability. A fish wine plus . . .

Chardonnay/Pinot Grigio Delle Venezie, Pasqua 1997 `15.5` `C`

Modern, fresh, flavourful but with a lovely crisp sense of its destiny: shellfish.

Frascati Superiore, Campoverdi 1997 `14` `C`

Indeed, it's a superior Frascati: dry yet with Italianate rococo hints.

La Bianchara Villa Lanata Chardonnay 1995

| 9 | D |

Oddly ineffective and muddy. Not to my taste at all. Cosmetic and tarty.

Moscato d'Asti, Bava 1997

| 15 | C |

A wonderfully scented, muscat-fruited, semi-bubbly of great warm-weather appetite-whetting wit.

Soave Classico, Santepietre 1997

| 14 | C |

It seems reluctant and even shy compared to new world fruit blitzkriegs but watch it motor with food . . . (spaghetti alla vongole, for example).

NEW ZEALAND WINE   RED

Delegat's Cabernet Merlot 1996

| 13 | D |

Linden Estate Merlot, Hawkes Bay 1995

| 13 | E |

NEW ZEALAND WINE   WHITE

Montana Sauvignon Blanc, Marlborough 1996

| 14.5 | D |

Nautilus Chardonnay, Marlborough 1995

| 15.5 | E |

Gentle creamy hint to the crisp fruit which is hard to classify. Shall I merely say it's deliciously *sui generis*?

Oyster Bay Chardonnay, Marlborough 1997   16   D

Raspberries, melons, lemons and hints of pineapple. It's all fruit – yet it's got finesse and elegance.

PORTUGUESE WINE   RED

Duas Quintas Tinto, Douro 1995   16   D

Makes a great change from cabernet or merlot. A beautifully polished wine, fleshy yet smooth, rich yet not overblown, it finishes with individuality and precision. Great price for such quality.

SOUTH AFRICAN WINE   RED

Drostdy-Hof Merlot 1996   13.5   D

Soft and juicy and a touch overpriced for such a simple affair.

**Kanonkop 'Paul Sauer' Cabernet
Sauvignon 1994**   13.5   G

Too expensive, even if it is highly accommodating to the taste buds.

Meerendal Pinotage 1995   15   D

Old fashioned as the metal studs in boot soles. A leathery, dry, hugely rich and deep pinotage of great character and uncompromising unctuosity.

Neil Ellis Cabernet Sauvignon 1994 12 E

Bit too juicy and ripe for me.

Two Oceans Cabernet Merlot 1997 15 C

Dry, wry, rich, deliciously lingering and fresh, yet it's got a lot of sly fruitiness which sneaks in unexpectedly (by virtue of the delivery system of the tannins).

SOUTH AFRICAN WINE WHITE

Blue Hills Chardonnay 1997 12 C

Somewhat muted.

De Wetshof Estate 'Lesca' Chardonnay 1997 14 D

Demure, quietly elegant, lemony.

Franschoek Barrel Fermented Chenin Blanc 1997 15.5 C

A more biting, more tenacious, more serious chenin. Has real oomph, complexity and class.

Neil Ellis Chardonnay 1996 15.5 E

Warm, elegant, nicely furnished with all the right fittings (acid, fruit in balance etc) but overall it's the confidence the wine exhibits which gives it its style.

Swartland Steen 1997 14 C

A brightly chirpy chenin blanc, crisp and incisive.

SPANISH WINE   RED

Artadi Vinas de Gain Rioja Crianza 1995   [16] [E]

Superb class here. Ripeness, earthiness, richness, and a compelling lilt on the finish which the curious drinker will be unable to resist repeating many times.

Guelbenzu Evo Cabernet/Merlot, Navarra 1993   [13.5] [E]

Guelbenzu Jardin, Navarra 1996   [16] [C]

Freshness yet dryness, fullness yet elegance, loads of wallop here but also insouciance and style. Yes, it has a touch of country cloth about it but it's well tailored and finely woven.

Marques de Grinon Crianza, Rioja 1996   [16] [C]

This is sheer cheek and utter effrontery. Do the rest of the Riojans know what the Marques is up to? It's disgraceful: pure, liquid fruit with soft, earthy tannins made absurdly delicious and deep and selling for under a fiver. Extraordinary.

Marques de Grinon Dominio de Valdepusa Syrah 1996   [16.5] [E]

Puts to shame many a much-vaunted northern Rhone syrah. This specimen of the grape is beautifully developed and rich and the complexity of the finish is magisterial.

Marques de la Musa Tempranillo 1997   [14] [B]

Dry and drinkable, but needs food to get it really going.

Marques de Murrieta Rioja Reserva 1993 · 13.5 · E

Very ripe and eager. The finish is quirky and an acquired taste.

Muga Rioja Gran Reserva 1989 · 12 · F

Too dry and pricey for this palate (or pocket).

Muga Rioja Reserva 1994 · 14 · E

Very earthy and bright, rugged and rich.

Navajas Rioja 1997 · 16.5 · C

What a price for such generous fruit! It's tobacco-edged, rich, dry, full of fruit and flavour, and it finishes with a huge grin on its face. A wonderful warm companion here.

Tempranillo Vina Armantes, Calatayud 1996 · 14.5 · C

Burnt rubber and gunsmoke, what an explosive little number we have here! Brilliant with food.

SPANISH WINE · WHITE

Marques de la Musa, Viura Chardonnay 1997 · 13 · B

Touch soppy on the finish.

Vinas del Vero Barrel Fermented Chardonnay, Somontano 1996 · 15 · D

The Spanish way with chardonnay is not as vivacious as you

might suppose. This has elegance, bite, class and a freshness of some charm.

USA WINE RED

Bel Arbor Merlot, Fetzer 1995 `13` `D`

Beringer Californian Zinfandel 1995 `14.5` `D`

Soft and rich, savoury hints and a lovely ripe finish. A real softie.

Beringer Harmonie Pinot Noir/Gamay 1996 `13.5` `D`

Very juicy and savoury.

Calera Pinot Noir, Central Coast 1996 `13` `F`

Juicy, ripe, dry. Lot of money for clichés. It is drinkable, but I can't see it's eleven quids' worth of drinkability.

Ironstone Vineyards Highlands Merlot 1995 `16` `D`

What a long fuse on this superbly textured wine. It explodes with rich, plump fruit only after it reaches the throat and it descends with polish, aplomb and great richness. Very classy.

Jekel Sanctuary Cabernet Sauvignon 1995 `14` `E`

Sweet finishing but dry at heart. Very soft and rich.

Madrona Zinfandel 1994 `13.5` `C`

Very jammy. Good pie filling.

Mondavi Pinot Noir, Napa 1995   14   G

Excellent – has real pinot tightness, richness, perfume and truffley finish, with a hint of wild strawberry. Monsieur Baptiste Brunet please take note (instead of just taking the mickey).

USA WINE
WHITE

Beringer Appellation Fume Blanc 1996   16.5   D

Tremendous breadth of flavours here, running the gamut from vanilla and smokiness to a rich, spicy melon with a hint of ice cream or it may be custard. Don't be alarmed, however. It is serious, dry and darned good.

Beringer Californian Zinfandel Blush 1997   10   D

Beringer Vineyards Sauvignon Blanc 1996   15.5   D

Lovely butterscotch edge to the rich, elegant fruit as it strokes the taste buds, a finish of impact yet gentility.

Calera Chardonnay, Central Coast 1996   17   F

Intense, concentrated, very rich, beautifully textured, slightly grassy and sensual (even a touch feral), and superbly well kitted out to handle food – like a roast farmyard fowl.

Fetzer Viognier 1996   15.5   E

Kautz Ironstone Vineyards Obsession Symphony 1996   12   C

Lieb fans will lap it up! It is indeed fully perfumed and sweet.

Mondavi Fume Blanc, Napa Valley 1995 | 14 | F |

Deliciously crisp and vivid – touch pricey for these privileges, though.

FORTIFIED WINE

Blandy's 5 Year old Sercial | 15 | F |

Lustau Old East India Sherry | 15.5 | E |

Tastes like the sweetest old aunt you ever had vinified into a rich, brown, caramel-coated confection of infinite depth, texture and richness.

Mick Morris Rutherglen Liqueur Muscat (half bottle) | 17 | C |

A miraculously richly textured pud wine of axle-grease texture and creamy figginess. Huge, world class.

Taylor's LBV 1992 | 15.5 | F |

Has the grip of a good vintage port. Lovely figgy richness and the sweetness is complex and vivid.

Taylor's Quinta de Vargellas 1984 | 13.5 | G |

SPARKLING WINE/CHAMPAGNE

Ayala Champagne NV | 13 | G |

Bollinger Grande Annee 1989 | 9.5 | H

I simply don't find it a thrill to drink and surely at nigh on forty quid it should be. Poor value bubbly, of little appeal to this curmudgeon.

Bouvet Ladubay Saumur NV (France) | 14.5 | E

Cava Verano, Freixenet NV | 15.5 | C

Dry, crisp, classic. Fantastic bargain.

De Telmont Grande Reserve Champagne NV | 13 | G

Gloria Ferrer Blanc de Noirs NV (California) | 15.5 | E

Hugely elegant with beautiful restrained fruit.

Gloria Ferrer Brut, Sonoma County (California) | 16 | E

Such elegance, charm and classic toast-edged fruit make you feel luxurious inside. A brilliant bubbly under a tenner.

Hunter's Miru Miru 1995 (New Zealand) | 14 | F

Very elegant.

Jacquart 1990 (Champagne) | 13.5 | G

Jacquart Brut Mosaique Champagne NV | 13 | G

Expensive for the style.

Louis Roderer Quartet NV (California) | 14 | G

Moet's Shadow Creek Blanc de Noirs (USA) | 14 | E

Oeil de Perdrix Tradition NV
14 G

Perrier-Jouet 1990 (Champagne)
12 H

Taittinger NV
12 H

A light dry Champagne costing twice as much as its excitement
level justifies.

Yellowglen Pinot Noir Chardonnay NV (Australia)
14 E

Soft yet finishes crisply. An elegant bubbly of some charm.

ODDBINS

STEVE'S GOOD NEWS IS NO NEWS. THAT'S BAD
NEWS (FOR THE COMPETITION).

Last year, Tesco were said to be interested in buying Oddbins
from its owners Seagram. However, Seagram had put a £60
million price tag, it was alleged, on the chain and this had put
Tesco off. I also heard the suggestion from some gossips that
Majestic was also interested in buying Odders; then Sainsbury
was said to have pricked up its ears; then Thresher; then Victoria
Wine; then Wine Cellar; and so and so on. Only Mr Richard
Branson, as a potential purchaser of the whole chain (as opposed
to the odd bottle), never entered the picture.

Six months later, seemingly indifferent to all these rumoured
marriages (some patently absurd and untrue), Oddbins opened
its first trial warehouse at Reading – selling wines at 'warehouse
prices'. The company says it is a trial. I am suspicious of this
word. Oddbins began as a trial: half a shop in the early sixties
in Agatha Christie's Seven Dials district (now subsumed under
the common appellation of Covent Garden). When is this trial
going to stop?

Personally, if I had sixty million smackers lying around idle,
I'd cheerfully stick it on Oddbins – on the nose. I also reckon
Tesco would, too. It wasn't the price as such which put Tesco
off, it was the property valuation. Supermarkets balance very
carefully the value of retail sites and if they don't make sense
to their way of looking at life, then they feel squeamish.

Yet what a brand name Oddbins represents. It could be the
name on the leading own-label wines in the UK, scores of them

from every wine region in the world, but no-one with the right financial clout to exploit this to the full has the wit or the vision to take the plunge (least of all Oddbins itself which prefers things the way they are: cosy and wine-grower label dominated except for the odd bin here and there like the Steadman labelled Oddbins Red). The nearest Oddbins got to this sort of idea is when it offered a mail-order case of wine, summer whites, for under £40 delivered. What made the case stand out, apart from the uniform consistency of the fruit (six different wines, two bottles of each) was the fact that each was guaranteed free from cork taint. The corks were plastic. Did my heart rejoice? It rejoiced.

Mr Steve Daniel, who is the guru who makes so many shrewd purchasing decisions for Oddbins, likes it, however, when there is no news. No news, that is, except for matters firmly connected to the stupendous range of wines, or prices, or regions, which other wine chains can only envy for its breadth, depth, and oft whackiness. That's always the best news of all for Oddbins customers. Nothing changes, except the wines are different vintages, there is an emphasis on the most individual wines of each region, and there is the odd daring raid on an area of neglect or underdogginess (like Greece). Well, I suppose the opening of an Oddbins so-called Mega-Store on Glasgow's Crow Road this last July was news of a sort.

The only real hard-and-fast news from the gossip front in 1998 at Oddbins was the defection of Miss Katie MacAulay, fine wine buying manager for the chain, to Bibendum. I do not write on Bibendum very often and I mourn the fact. This wine merchant is intent on snapping up the most able people in the wine trade (it nabbed the astonishing Miss Helen Sugarman, now Mrs Nathan, from BRL Hardy a while back) and somehow persuading them to work just along the road from elegant Primrose Hill and proximate to the raffish purlieu of Chalk Farm; other merchants must wonder what is put in the interview tea.

Oddbins, of course, will simply go on as it always has done. Good luck, Katie.

Oddbins
31–32 Weir Road
Wimbledon
London SW19 8UG
Tel: 0181 944 4400
Fax: 0181 944 4411

SEE STOP PRESS SECTION AT END OF BOOK FOR LAST-MINUTE ADDITIONS OR UPDATES TO THIS RETAILER'S RANGE.

ARGENTINIAN WINE RED

Balbi Vineyards Malbec 1997 14 C

Juicy and rich, as all Balbi's wines seem to be. It bounces around the taste buds like a big bonny bowl of fruit (dryish).

Flichman Caballero de la Cepa Cabernet Sauvignon 1995 15.5 E

Tannins smoothing themselves out and relaxing with the equally well developed fruit.

Flichman Cabernet Sauvignon, Mendoza 1997 15.5 C

Oh boy! Knocks spots off claret at three times the price.

Flichman Malbec, Mendoza 1997 15.5 C

Lovely character: dry, whiskery, rich. Great with food.

Flichman Merlot, Mendoza 1997 16 C

Superb rolling richness and earthiness. Great smoothie yet craggy individualist.

Flichman Syrah, Mendoza 1995 14 D

Touch of austerity about the tannins, but they hang in there, and the fruit is in full flow.

Flichman Tempranillo, Mendoza 1997 `14` `C`

Good dry glugging.

Isla Negra Bonarda, Mendoza 1997 `15` `C`

Rich and juicy and an alternative to overpriced Beaujolais.

Isla Negra Malbec, Mendoza 1997 `15` `D`

Classic Argentine malbec, it seems to me: juicy and ripe yet dry.

Isla Negra Syrah, Mendoza 1997 `16.5` `D`

More rampant than any Aussie for the same money. Terrific style here.

Marques de Grinon Dom Agrelo Malbec, Mendoza 1996 `16` `D`

A very stylish malbec. Has perfume, presence, persistence, loads of flavour, dryness and depth, and a finish of considerable finesse yet weight.

Marques de Grinon Duarte Malbec, Mendoza 1996 `15` `C`

Juicy and ripe with an earthen edge.

Norton Cabernet Sauvignon, Mendoza 1994 `16` `D`

What astonishingly well-polished, integrated fruit and tannins here. Beautifully velvety and posh.

Norton Malbec, Mendoza 1994 `14.5` `D`

Curiously delicious edge to this deliciously smooth fruit.

Norton Merlot, Mendoza 1994

Juicy and very ripely smooth and unhurried.

Norton Privada, Mendoza 1996

Love its rich flamboyance and concentration. It's a meat sauce of a wine!

Norton Reserve Cabernet Sauvignon, Mendoza 1997

Suggestion of custard and fine tobacco here. Odd? Yes, but compelling and very delicious.

Norton Reserve Malbec, Mendoza 1997

Great complexity of tonal fruit flavours here. Textured, ripe, untroubled, calm, very classy.

Norton Reserve Syrah Cabernet, Mendoza 1997

Superb tannins and plummily rich fruit.

Valentin Bianchi Elsa's Vineyard Cabernet Sauvignon, Mendoza 1993

Stands close to the pinnacle of Argentine cabs: the tannins are inspirations.

Valentin Bianchi Malbec, San Rafael 1996

Softly ripe and flavoursome.

Valentin Bianchi Reserve Malbec 1995

Extraordinary specimen of jammy richness and mingled tannic

softness. Strikingly deep and gooey, it nevertheless has some gauche charm. Great for big rich casseroles.

ARGENTINIAN WINE WHITE

Norton Torrontes 1997

Brilliant food wine: loads of flavour and strength of purpose.

AUSTRALIAN WINE RED

Angove's Classic Reserve Cabernet Sauvignon 1996

Juicy quaffability. Rich and ready.

Angove's Classic Reserve Shiraz 1996

Simply, it's Australia at the right price with the right soupy dryness and sunny, rich characterfulness. Sensuous, ripe, fun, this is what it's all about: sheer textured pleasure.

Annie's Lane Cabernet Merlot 1996

Deliciously rich and well polished.

Campbells Bobbie Burns Shiraz, Rutherglen 1996

Hugely rampaging yet soft fruit here, like being trampled by a herd of chamois.

Chateau Reynella Basket-Pressed Shiraz 1995

| 15.5 | F |

Cassis and tannins. What a recipe for heavenly quaffing. Pity the price has gone astronomic, though.

Coldstream Hills Reserve Cabernet, Yarra Valley 1995

| 13.5 | G |

Cranswick Estate John's Vineyard Grenache, Riverina 1996

| 13 | D |

So much juice!

Cranswick Estate Nine Pines Vineyard Cabernet Merlot, Riverina 1996

| 13.5 | D |

Juicy and a bit jammy on the finish. The tannins are crushed.

---

d'Arenberg Red Ochre, McLaren Vale 1996

| 13.5 | C |

---

d'Arenberg The Custodian Grenache, McLaren Vale 1996

| 15.5 | E |

Loads of rich flavour here with complexity and gentle wallop. Great style for soft fruit lovers.

---

d'Arenberg The Footbolt Old Vine Shiraz, McLaren Vale 1996

| 13.5 | D |

Yet more juice.

---

d'Arenberg The High Trellis Cabernet Sauvignon, McLaren Vale 1996

| 15 | D |

High class fruit soup with attendant tannins nicely impolite.

Deakin Estate Cabernet Sauvignon, Victoria 1997

14 | C

Juicy and delicious with a hint of strawberry jam and tobacco.

Hardys Banrock Station Shiraz 1997

13.5 | D

Merrill's Mount Hurtle Bush Vine Grenache, McLaren Vale 1996

13.5 | D

Very juicy.

Mount Helen Cabernet Merlot 1996

14.5 | E

Juicy and jammy but with delightful tannins and acidity.

Mount Hurtle Grenache Shiraz 1996

14 | C

Not every day you find an Aussie red so juicy and ripe yet so amenable to food costing under a fiver.

Mount Ida Shiraz 1996

15 | E

Exuberant and very cheeky yet with a dry, tannic undertone of class and precision.

Norman Bin C106 Cabernet Sauvignon, 1995

13.5 | D

Normans Lone Gum Shiraz/Cabernet Sauvignon 1997

12 | C

Juice all the way.

Penfolds Rawson's Retreat Bin 35 1996

13 | C

Peter Lehmann Cabernet Sauvignon, Barossa 1996

16.5 | E

Superb texture where the fruit and the tannins are eager, smooth and beautifully polished. Aussie cab sauv as a really suave beast.

Peter Lehmann Clancy's Red 1996

14.5 | E

Juicy yet the tannins kick in deliciously before the sensation's over.

Peter Lehmann The Seven Surveys Grenache Shiraz Mourvedre 1996

15 | D

Indeed dry and wry, fresh, fleshy, yet has tannin and backbone.

Peter Lehmann Vine Vale Grenache, Barossa 1997

14.5 | C

Sticky fruit of great adhesive character where food is concerned. Hums with fruit.

Riddoch Coonawarra Cabernet Shiraz 1995

13 | D

Saltram Stonyfell Metala, Langhorne Creek 1995

13.5 | D

Seppelt Terrain Series Cabernet Sauvignon 1996

14 | D

The juice has got tannin! So it's got character!

Seppelt Terrain Series Shiraz 1996

11.5 | D

Tatachilla Langhorne Creek Cabernet Sauvignon 1996

14.5 | E

Ripeness, richness, softness but no soppiness. The tannins roll around nicely.

Tatachilla Wattle Park Shiraz/Cabernet Sauvignon 1997

12 | D

More juice.

Yarra Valley Hills Cabernet Sauvignon 1996

15 | F

Interesting version of claret here. The peppery and vegetal cabernet has plum sauce poured over it. Rather splendid – if disconcerting.

AUSTRALIAN WINE   WHITE

Annie's Lane Chardonnay, Clare Valley 1997

15 | D

Rather classy yet ripe, dry, full and deep. Lovely woody tang on the finish.

Annie's Lane Riesling, Clare Valley 1997

13.5 | D

Needs a couple of years in bottle.

Bethany Riesling, Barossa 1997

15.5 | C

Wonderfully rich riesling of advanced deliciousness. However, in two or three years it'll be even better.

Bethany the Manse Dry White, Barossa 1997

14 C

Curiously unAussie-style dryness to the ripeness.

Cambells Rutherglen Liqueur Muscat (half bottle)

16 D

Superb depth of raisiny richness and sweetness. A wondrous accompaniment to rich cake.

Cranswick Estate Zirilli Vineyard Botrytis Semillon, Riverina 1996

16.5 E

Medicinal, thick, rich, very sweet but with the textured fruit so well served by the brilliant acidity.

---

d'Arenberg Noble Riesling, McLaren Vale 1996 (half bottle)

14.5 E

Sweetly engaging. Needs fresh fruit to really set it off.

Deakin Estate Chardonnay, Victoria 1997

16 C

Unusual to find an under-a-fiver Aussie chardonnay so couth, civilised, classy and utterly delicious. Lovely texture and ripe, plump fruit.

James Halliday Botrytis Semillon 1996 (half bottle)

16.5 D

Superb waxy sweet fruit with thrilling toffee-nosed rotten grapes giving it breadth, depth and luxuriousness.

Jamiesons Run Chardonnay, Coonawarra 1996

13 E

Bit uncertain on the finish.

Jim Barry Lodge Hill Riesling, Clare Valley 1996

12 E

Rather numb.

Killawarra Dry White

15 B

Knappstein Riesling, Clare Valley 1997

13.5 D

Lindemans Bin 65 Chardonnay 1997

16 C

One of the most elegant of Aussie chardonnays. Gorgeous, rich, knock-out.

Lindemans Cawarra Unoaked Chardonnay 1997

15 C

Shows the impressive richness and balance of Aussie's fruit unadulterated by wood. Delicious flavours here.

Normans Bin C207 Chardonnay 1996

15.5 C

Normans Chardonnay Bin 207 1996

15 D

Wonderful freshness yet richness. A cataract of rolling, fresh fruit.

Penfolds Old Vine Semillon, Barossa 1997

14 D

I'd be inclined to leave it for another eighteen months. It might rate 16/17.

Penfolds Rawsons Retreat Bin 21 Semillon Chardonnay Colombard 1997

15 C

Seemingly casually attired at first meeting, it reveals some jazzy habiliments as it progresses from nose to throat.

Penfolds The Valley Chardonnay 1996 | 14 | D

Insouciance, charm, casual but stylish richness.

Penfolds Trial Bin Adelaide Hills Chardonnay 1995 | 13 | F

Petaluma Chardonnay, Piccadilly Valley 1996 | 14 | G

Like a glum Puligny.

Peter Lehmann Clancy's Chardonnay Semillon, Barossa Valley 1996 | 16 | D

Rich and rampant yet never overdone. A lovely food wine.

Peter Lehmann Eden Valley Riesling 1997 | 14 | D

Good oriental food wine. Will develop over the next year.

Peter Lehmann Semillon, Barossa Valley 1997 | 16 | D

Gorgeous display of two-faced insidiously delicious fruit. Has soft, erotic ripe fruit on one hand and a rippling mineral acidity on the other.

Pewsey Vale Riesling, Eden Valley 1997 | 15 | D

Rich, quirky, fresh, deeply flavoured, gorgeous.

Saltram Mamre Brook Chardonnay 1996 | 15.5 | D

Always a stalwart chardonnay, this is typically rich and full of flavour, but this vintage seems more delicate than others. More impressive, curiously. Not so taste bud busting.

W W Chardonnay, McLaren Vale 1996 | 13.5 | C

Yarra Valley Hills Chardonnay 1997 | 14 | E

Lot of dosh but a lot of class. Impressively woody as it gathers itself for the final assault on the throat.

Yarra Valley Riesling 1997 | 14 | D

Needs Thai food – *now*!

BULGARIAN WINE   RED

Stowells of Chelsea Bulgarian Red (3-litre box) | 11 | B

Price bracket has been adjusted to show bottle equivalent.

CHILEAN WINE   RED

Carmen Merlot, Central Valley 1997 | 15 | C

Very dry and cheroot-edged. Delicious wine for food.

Carmen Reserve Cabernet Sauvignon, Maipo 1996 | 15.5 | D

It's the texture which makes it such a bargain. The fruit is like plums made from smoky velvet.

Carmen Reserve Grande Vidure Cabernet, Maipo 1996
15 D

Juicy yet classy and full of flavour. Plastic cork.

Casa Lapostolle Cuvee Alexandre Merlot, Rapel 1996
17 E

One of Chile's most stunning merlots: thick, plaited tannin and leathery fruit, and a richness of fruit which defies the price tag. Petrus? Forget it.

Casa Porta Cabernet Sauvignon 1996
16 C

The rich fruit has a black, mysterious, almost charcoal edge to it (tannins). It's lovely.

Concha y Toro 'Explorer' Bouschet, Maule 1996

Concha y Toro Explorer Cabernet/Syrah, Maipo 1996
17 C

Makes you limp with pleasure. World class texture, balance, depth and length and . . . price. Fabulous stuff!

Cono Sur Selection Reserve Cabernet Sauvignon, Chimbarongo 1995

Errazuriz Cabernet Sauvignon 1996
16 D

Utter balm! Sheer textured brilliance from nose to throat and beyond (i.e. the soupy richness of the wine lingers in the mind).

Errazuriz Merlot 1996   17 | D

Totally delicious: textured, dry, multi-layered, gently leathery and enticingly aromatic, rich yet not forbidding, stylish, very classy and overwhelmingly terrific value for money.

Isla Negra Cabernet Sauvignon, Rapel 1997   17 | C

Such unencumbered fruit! It's pure, rich, dry, exuberant yet very classy. The texture is superb.

La Palma Cabernet Sauvignon, Rapel 1996   15.5 | C

Quiet but deadly effective: dry, rich, stylish.

La Palma Merlot 1997   16 | C

Gorgeous concentration of leathery softness and almost jammy sweetness but not in fact sugary because of the complexity of the finish. Lovely stuff.

La Palma Reserve Cabernet Sauvignon/ Merlot, Rapel 1996   16 | C

A real Chilean food wine: rich, dry, fully formed and throaty.

Medalla Real Santa Rita Cabernet Sauvignon 1995   16.5 | D

Depth, width, length, angularity, roundedness, and it's not square. What a shape for a cabernet!

Morande Aventura Bouschet 1997   14 | C

Delightfully exuberant and fumaciously inclined.

Morande Aventura Carignan 1997   13.5   C

Needs food, try Indian.

Morande Aventura Cesar 1997   13   C

Bit too sulphurous for me.

Morande Aventura Cinsault 1997   13.5   C

Fresh and fruity, simple.

Morande Aventura Malbec 1997   13   C

Expensive for the lushness of the style.

**Pupilla Luis Felipe Edwards Cabernet
Sauvignon 1997**   16.5   C

Captivating and haunting stuff. Has a lovely textured ripeness
but the tone of the thing as it descends, and then lingers, is like
Bach on the organ.

**Santa Rita Reserve Cabernet Sauvignon
1995**   15.5   D

Santa Rita Reserve Merlot 1996   16   D

Compelling richness and texture, classy fruit, longevity of finish
and delicious, serious balance of elements.

**Veramonte Cabernet Sauvignon, Alto de
Casablanca 1997**   16   D

Oddly well-developed, almost precociously so, for such young
wine . . . but what wit this baby produces!

Veramonte Merlot, Alto de Casablanca 1997

`14.5` `D`

Very juicy and richly flowing.

Villa Montes Cabernet Sauvignon, Curico 1996

`15` `C`

Villa Montes Malbec, Colchagua 1996

`15.5` `C`

Vina Porta Merlot 1996

`16` `D`

Leathery as young bootees and almost as raunchy.

Vina Porta Reserva Unfiltered Cabernet Sauvignon 1995

`17` `E`

Utterly stunningly savoury cabernet with tannins, tenacity and sublime typicity.

CHILEAN WINE   WHITE

Andes Peaks Chardonnay, Casablanca 1997

`13.5` `C`

Andes Peaks Sauvignon Blanc 1997

`15` `C`

Excellent varietal character with hints of gooseberry, raspberry and nuts. Delicious aperitif.

Carmen Reserve Chardonnay, Central Valley 1997

`16.5` `D`

Wonderful richness and concentration here. Superb class too.

Casa Lapostolle Cuvee Alexandre Chardonnay 1997

| 17 | E |

One of Chile's greatest chardonnays. Has superb balance (richness, ripeness, length of flavour) and it's so classy it hurts.

Casa Lapostolle Sauvignon Blanc 1997

| 16 | C |

Casa Porta Chardonnay, Cachapoal 1997

| 15.5 | C |

Rich melon and gentle lemon fruit. Well mannered but not entirely mild.

Casablanca White Label Sauvignon Blanc, Curico 1997

| 15.5 | D |

A lovely smoked fish and shellfish wine.

Errazuriz Chardonnay, La Escultura Estate Casablanca 1997

| 16 | D |

Fabulous richness of attack with emulsion-thick melon fruit piling it on! Terrific pace to this wine in spite of the weight.

Errazuriz Reserve Chardonnay 1996

| 16 | E |

Errazuriz Sauvignon Blanc, La Escultura Estate Casablanca 1997

| 14 | C |

Has richness and concentration.

La Palma Chardonnay 1997

| 16 | C |

So winningly textured and warmly fruity for the money one is given cause for disbelief. A lovely, rich, classy, deep yet delicate mouthful.

Santa Carolina Sauvignon Blanc 1997 `15.5` `C`

Veramonte Chardonnay, Casablanca 1997 `15` `D`

Food and mood both go well with it: quiet class shines through it all.

Villard Casablanca Vineyard Chardonnay, Aconcagua 1995 `15` `D`

Vina Casablanca Santa Isabel Barrel Fermented Chardonnay, Casablanca 1997 `14` `E`

Seems a touch expensive for the fruit which is not as exciting as other Chilean chardonnays at half the price. It may be it needs another eighteen months in bottle.

Vina Casablanca Santa Isabel Chardonnay, Casablanca 1997 `15.5` `D`

Soft yet crisp, flavoursome yet subtle, muscular yet lithe. A lovely contradiction.

Vina Casablanca Sauvignon Blanc, Lontue 1997 `16.5` `D`

What wonderful oily texture, richness yet elegance of finish, what terrific underlying nuttiness! A terrific wine.

FRENCH WINE RED

Banyuls Les Clos de Paulilles 1993 `16.5` `E`

Sweet, pruney, honeyed, blackcurrant-and-raspberry-and-plum

scented, this is a terrific wine for fruit cake. Fine Wine Shops only.

Chateau Close Bellevue, Cru Bourgeois Medoc 1996

15.5   D

A classic claret but with, astonishingly, a warm, herby edge to the finish. Lovely stuff.

Chateau de Nages Reserve du Chateau, Costieres de Nimes 1997

16   C

Charcoal, old cigar butts, earth, all coating gorgeous plum fruit. Character, style and richness here.

Chateau de Parenchere Cuvee Raphael Gazaniol, Bordeaux Superieure 1995

15   E

Lovely claret of wit and weight, taste bud hugging tannins.

Chateau de Passedieu, Cotes de Bourg 1996

14   C

A very dry food wine. Great with rare roast meats.

Chateau Lousteauneuf, 1995

14   D

Chateau Rollan de By, Cru Bourgeois Medoc 1995

13   E

Chateau Vaugelas Corbieres Cuvee Prestige 1995

16   C

Classy and rich with a touch of flamboyance on the edge as it finishes. Dry, fruity, lovely.

Chinon Domaine de la Perriere 1996

15.5   D

Cotes du Rhone Guigal 1994 15 D

Crozes Hermitage Cuvee Louis Belle, Belle Pere et Fils 1995 16.5 E

Lovely authentic Crozes which smells of charcoal and farm compost (of the sweet variety) and offers fruity dryness, depth, decisiveness and daring. Swashbuckling stuff.

Cuvee de Grignon VdP de l'Aude 1997 14 B

Simply fruity stuff on one level with hints of earth.

James Herrick Cuvee Simone VdP d'Oc 1995 13.5 C

Le Secret VdP de Vaucluse 1996 14 B

Mas Saint-Vincent Coteaux du Languedoc 1997 15.5 C

Lovely rich tannin and earthy dryness with such biteable fruit teasing the edge.

Metairie du Bois Syrah VdP d'Oc 1996 14 C

Oddbins Red VdP d'Oc 1996 15.5 C

Getting more elegant, this own-label Oddbin. But it's still rich, characterful, and earthily delicious.

Parallel '45' Cotes du Rhone 1995 14.5 D

Ptomaine de Blageurs Syrah, VdP d'Oc 1996 14 C

Rather mild fruit for so extravagant a jokey, farty title.

Ptomaine de Blageurs Vin de Table 1996 `13` `C`

**Stowells of Chelsea Vin de Pays du Gard
(3-litre box)** `13.5` `B`

Price bracket has been adjusted to show bottle equivalent.

Wild Pig Red, VdP d'Oc 1997 `15` `B`

Delicious cherry fruit. Great value, chilled, with or without
food.

Wild Pig Shiraz VdP d'Oc 1997 `15.5` `C`

For seventy pence more you get seventy pence more spice and
edgy earthiness.

FRENCH WINE WHITE

**Cave Saint Prix 'Portlandien' Sauvignon de
St Bris 1996** `15` `C`

Gorgeous grassy fruit. A terrific fish wine.

Chateau de l'Hospital Blanc, Graves 1996 `13` `E`

**Chateau de la Genaiserie Coteaux du
Layon, Yves Soulez 1997** `16` `D`

Wonderfully rich aperitif with hints of honey and candied
pineapple. Delicious!

**Chateau de Nages Reserve du Chateau,
Costieres de Nimes Blanc 1997** `15` `C`

Lipsmacking fruitiness without blowsiness. Lovely!

Clos du Chateau Bourgogne, Domaine du Chateau de Puligny-Montrachet 1996 | 14 | E |

Real classy white burgundy under a tenner. Rich and sveltely textured.

Condrieu La Petite Cote, Cuilleron 1997 | 17 | G |

Wonderful dry apricots and sesame seed fruit – yet so dry and dainty! One of France's best white wine makers here on top form. Drink this in preference to many great white burgundies.

Cuvee de Grignon Blanc, VdP de l'Aude 1997 | 15.5 | B |

Brilliant richness and flavour.

Domaine Garras VdP des Cotes de Gascogne 1997 | 13.5 | B |

Cheerful and cheap.

Domaine Ournac Viognier, VdP d'Oc 1997 | 13 | C |

Domaine St Hilaire Chardonnay VdP d'Oc 1996 | 15 | C |

Gewurztraminer, Hugel 1995 | 12 | E |

Gewurztraminer Tradition, Hugel 1995 | 12 | F |

James Herrick Chardonnay VdP d'Oc 1996 | 15 | C |

Calm and classy. Perhaps more lemony than previous vintages. Limited distribution.

**La Baume Philippe de Baudin Chardonnay
VdP d'Oc 1995** `14.5` `C`

**Menetou Salon 'Clos Ratier', Domaine
Henry Pelle 1997** `14.5` `D`

Often a better bet than neighbouring Sancerre, this is a lovely
classy specimen of untrammelled fruit.

Michel Lynch Bordeaux Blanc 1997 `12.5` `D`

Muscat, Albert Mann 1997 `15` `E`

One of my favourite aperitifs: spicy and warm.

Pinot Blanc, Albert Mann 1997 `14.5` `D`

Fat and comfortable on the taste buds. Sits richly and firmly.

**Saumur Blanc, Chateau de Montgeuret
1996** `16` `C`

Gorgeous complexity: hints of gooseberry, asparagus and melon
with a hint of mineral acidity.

**Stowells of Chelsea Vin de Pays du Tarn
(3-litre box)** `14` `B`

Price bracket has been adjusted to show bottle equivalent.

Sylvaner, Albert Mann 1997 `16` `D`

Gorgeous, rich, exotic, never overdone. Great as an aperitif or
with Thai fish dishes.

**Tokay Pinot Gris Vieilles Vignes, Albert
Mann 1997** `15.5` `E`

Will develop into a more exciting wine over the next few years
but already shows its rich apricot fruitiness.

Touraine Sauvignon, Domaine de la Renaudie 1997

14 C

Nervous edge to the crisp fruit.

Vouvray 'Girardieres' Demi Sec, Domaine des Aubuisieres 1996

15 D

Vouvray 'Les Chairs Salees', Domaine des Aubuisieres 1996

14 D

Vouvray Moelleux Cuvee Alexandre, Domaine des Aubuisieres 1996

14 F

Give it ten years then watch it perform! It's a potential eighteen-pointer.

Vouvray Moelleux Les Girardieres 1ere Trie 1996

15 G

Lovely richness here of honeyed hard fruit. But will age well for years. Potentially nineteen points.

GERMAN WINE   WHITE

'Armand' Riesling Kabinett, Von Buhl Pfalz 1996

11 E

Can't rate it any higher – for now. It might be better in a hundred years. I should care.

Bechtheimer Hasensprung Huxelrebe Spatlese, Wittmann, Rheinhessen 1996

13.5 D

Kendermann K Vineyards Riesling, Rheingau 1996

Is it sweet? Is it dry? Is it louche? Is it wry? Even the wine doesn't know.

Messmer Burrweiler Altenforst Scheurebe Spatlese 1997

Spicy grapefruit and a hint of orange. Suggest you wait until 2006 for this to be *really* dazzling.

Messmer Burrweiler Schlossgarten Riesling Kabinett Halbtrocken 1997

Bit reluctant. Won't necessarily become more giving with age.

Messmer Muller-Thurgau, Pfalz 1996

Rotten value at a fiver. And it's sort of fruity, sweetish and impossibly sentimental.

Schultz-Werner Gaubischhofheimer Herrenberg Riesling Kabinett, Rheinhessen 1997

Don't drink it now. Wait five years. Tough, but there it is.

Von Buhl Forster Jesuitengarten Riesling Spatlese, Pfalz 1997

So much texture and vigour Von Buhl gets in young rieslings! Yet in ten years' time will this wine rate 19 points?!

Von Buhl Forster Kirchenstuck Riesling Spatlese, Pfalz 1997

Wonderful richness and tonal complexity here. Drink it with oriental food or watching the Hang Seng index on a screen.

Von Buhl Riesling Kabinett Trocken, Pfalz 1996   `12` `D`

Westhofner Kirchspiel Scheurebe Kabinett, Wittman, Rheinhessen 1997   `14` `D`

Hint of sweet grapefruit but even so I'd age it for 24 months more.

GREEK WINE   RED

Boutari Agioritiko, Nemea 1994   `15.5` `E`

Very dry and earthy to finish with hints of chocolate, cassis and wood. Great with food.

Gaia Notios Red, Peloponnese 1997   `15` `D`

Wonderful ripe tannins and richness to the fruit. Most individual.

Ktima Kosta Lazaridis Amethystos Red, Drama 1997   `16` `E`

Claret meets Amarone. An oddly delicious dry yet ripe wine of quirkiness and style.

Papantonis Miden Agan, Peloponnese 1996   `16` `E`

Delicious rich tannins here with a warmth and richness of some class. Comes across like a terrific quirky claret.

Spiropoulos Porfyros, Peloponnese 1996   `14` `D`

Soft light quaffing wine with a hint of wild scrub.

Strofilia Red, Peloponnese 1994 15.5 D

Rampant richness and gently exotic fruit. Brilliant spicy food wine.

GREEK WINE   WHITE

Antonopolous Chardonnay, Peloponnese 1997 14 E

Lovely wine for a Greek *meze*. But what a price to pay for such vanillary subtleties!

Boutari Visanto, Santorini 1993 (50cl) 16 D

Unusual pudding wine with hints of nuts, honey, melon. Yet, curiously, it finishes like dry apple skin.

Gaia Notios White, Peloponnese 1997 13 C

Nervous.

Ktima Kosta Lazaridis Amethystos White, Drama 1997 14 D

Great food wine. Rich yet crisp.

Spiropoulos Manitinia Dry White, Peloponnese 1997 13 C

Bit wrinkled on the edges.

Strofilia White, Peloponnese 1997 14.5 C

Has self evident class. Great!

**Tselepos Barrique Chardonnay, Arcadia
1997** 13.5 E

Interesting creamy, woody finish. Lot of dosh though.

Tselepos Moschofilero, Mantinia 1997 13 D

Bit one-dimensional for this price.

ITALIAN WINE RED

Bricco Zanone Barbera d'Asti 1995 14 C

**Duca di Castelmonte Cent'are Rosso
1996 (Sicily)** 15 C

Soft and jammy with rich ripe tannins. Great glugging here.

Due Aquile 14 B

**Notarpanaro Rosso del Salento, Taurino
1990** 14.5 D

Salice Salento, Vallone 1994 16.5 C

Big, brothy, savoury, coffee undertones swirling through a rich,
soft-fruit centre of soft ripeness, this is a lovely glug.

Santa Barbara Brindisi Rosso 1993 14 C

**Torre Veneto Torre del Falco, Murgia
Rosso 1995** 14 D

Torre Vento Primitivo del Tarantino 1996 | 13.5 | C |

Needs food. Very fresh, overripe, raisiny.

ITALIAN WINE WHITE

Torcolato, Maculan 1995 | 16.5 | G |

Nuts, honey, pineapples, melons, pears, limes – is there a fruit not represented here? A world-class dessert wine which will age for a decade – and then some.

NEW ZEALAND WINE RED

McDonald Church Road Reserve Merlot, Hawkes Bay 1996 | 14 | F |

Luxury leather interior, nice red paintwork (no flashy chrome), this limousine of a wine purrs with a vintage growl yet takes you from nose to throat with a touch of ordinariness which is at variance with the style of the setting off.

Montana Fairhall Estate Cabernet Sauvignon, Marlborough 1996 | 13 | F |

Minty, pert, fruity, yet wildly overpriced. A five quid wine.

Montana Reserve Barrique Matured Merlot, Marlborough 1996 | 13 | E |

Bit too juicy for the lolly.

Villa Maria Cabernet Merlot, Hawkes Bay 1996

`14` `E`

Very juicy with hints of plum and blackcurrant. Touch expensive for so simplistic an expression.

NEW ZEALAND WINE WHITE

Jackson Estate Sauvignon Blanc 1997

`16` `E`

Richness, texture, ripeness, real class, finish, polish, wit and consummate drinkability.

Montana Chardonnay, Marlborough 1997

`14.5` `D`

Crisp and well-finished, nothing herbaceous or overly vegetal. An excellent fish wine.

Montana Reserve Barrique Fermented Chardonnay, Marlborough 1997

`14.5` `E`

Classy richness with a slightly uncertain, vanillary finish.

Montana Reserve Riesling, Awatere Valley 1997

`16` `E`

Stunning richness and flattering fruit – it compliments you on your good taste with every drop.

Montana Reserve Sauvignon Blanc, Marlborough 1997

`15` `E`

Beautifully controlled grassiness.

Montana Sauvignon Blanc 1997 `15` `D`

Lovely rich grass to gnaw on here. A ruminative wine.

Selaks Sauvignon Blanc 1996 `15.5` `D`

**Stowells of Chelsea New Zealand
Sauvignon Blanc (3-litre box)** `13.5` `C`

Price bracket has been adjusted to show bottle equivalent.

**Villa Maria Cellar Selection Sauvignon
Blanc, Marlborough 1997** `16` `E`

The acme of modern sauvignon where richness and grassiness combine superbly.

**Villa Maria Private Bin Chardonnay,
Marlborough 1997** `14` `D`

Young (and it will improve) but very rich and ready to provide lingering fruity pleasures.

PORTUGUESE WINE
RED

Caves Alianca Palmela, Douro 1996 `15` `C`

Wonderful broth of wine: savoury, soft, dry to finish, characterful.

Pegos Claros, Palmela 1993 `16.5` `E`

Boot polish, leather and tobacco plus a hint of spice, rich hedgerow fruit and tannin.

Quinta da Lagoalva, Ribatejo 1994 `16` `D`

Lovely ripeness yet dryness here. Explodes, yet it's chic and stylish.

Terra Boa Vinho Regional 1996 `12.5` `B`

PORTUGUESE WINE WHITE

Segada Branco, Ribatejo 1997 `14` `C`

Rich, dry, soft and singular fatty fruit of softness and style.

SOUTH AFRICAN WINE RED

Beyerskloof Pinotage 1997 `14` `D`

Fresh and boot polishy.

Blaauwklippen Cabernet Sauvignon/Merlot `13.5` `C`

Juicy fruit.

Blaauwklippen Shiraz, Stellenbosch 1995 `16` `D`

Wonderful rich sense of fun to this wine yet under it all it's serious. Savoury, tobacco-edged fruit here.

Clos Malverne Pinotage 1996 `16` `D`

Wonderfully invigorating and enticing bouquet of chestnuts roasting and cedar wood-smoke. The fruit is less complex and juicier than anticipated but still impressive. Will age interestingly for two years.

Clos Malverne Pinotage Reserve 1996 `16.5` `E`

Gorgeous length of flavour here. It develops nuances for half a minute after the wine has descended the throat. It's rich, ripely textured, and completely gripping.

Delheim Shiraz, Stellenbosch 1996 `13` `D`

Tobacco juice.

Fairview Zinfandel Cinsault 1997 `16` `D`

Simply a gorgeous glug. Such exuberance yet class, it's lovely yet battle hardened.

Jacana Cabernet Sauvignon/Shiraz/Merlot, Stellenbosch 1996 `14` `D`

Jacques Kruger Cabernet Sauvignon, Stellenbosch 1995 `13` `E`

Very juicy.

John Goschen Cabernet Sauvignon, Coastal Region 1996 `15` `E`

Most unusual: herby, ripe, fresh, tobaccoey, yet inexpressibly cheeky and chic.

Ken Forrester Grenache/Syrah 1996 `10` `C`

Don't like it more than 10. Too gooey.

Louisvale Cabernet, Stellenbosch 1996 `13` `D`

Savanha Shiraz, Western Cape 1996 13.5 C

Sentinel Shiraz, Stellenbosch 1997 13 D

Bit too juicy for me at this price.

Veenwouden Merlot, Paarl 1996 13 F

Too pricey.

Veenwouden Vivat Bacchus, Paarl 1996 13 E

Lot of money for juice, however elegant.

Wildekrans Cabernet Franc/Merlot, Walker Bay 1997 13.5 D

Wildekrans Cabernet Sauvignon, Walker Bay 1996 13 E

Soupy.

SOUTH AFRICAN WINE WHITE

Collingbourne Cape White 14 B

Danie de Wet Chardonnay Sur Lie 1997 14 C

Flavour and style here, albeit not as gripping nor as elegant as previous vintages.

De Wetshof Estate Reserve Selection Bon Vallon Chardonnay 1997 15.5 D

Very very elegant and relaxed. Has an insouciant charm.

Eikendal Chardonnay, Stellenbosch 1997   15 | D

Quiet but determined. Gentle creaminess of fruit.

Fair Valley Bush Vine Chenin 1998   15.5 | C

The first worker-owned vineyard in S.A. Plastic cork too!
Lovely rich nuttiness with a surging freshness underneath.
Lovely stuff.

Fairview Chardonnay, Paarl 1997   15.5 | D

It's that lovely rich and creamy finish, almost yoghurty, which
is so charming.

Glen Carlou Chardonnay, Paarl 1997   14 | E

Lot of money for the style which needs time to reluctantly show
its class as it descends.

Jacana Chardonnay, Stellenbosch 1996   15.5 | D

Louisvale Wooded Chardonnay 1995   14.5 | D

Scholzenhof Ken Forrester Barrel Reserve
Chenin Blanc, Stellenbosch 1996   14 | D

Sentinel Chardonnay 1997   16 | D

Deeply classy and woody but the fruit calls the shots over
the wood.

Southern Right Sauvignon Blanc 1997   14 | D

Vergelegen Reserve Chardonnay 1996   16.5 | E

Lovely, lovely wine of great class.

Villiera Estate Blue Ridge Sauvignon Blanc 1996

Lovely creamy richness perfectly offset by a crisp, fruity undertone.

SPANISH WINE   RED

Castillo de Monjardin Tinto Joven, Navarra 1996

Great value here. Has lovely depth and flavour and great soft texture.

Condado de Haza, Ribera del Duero 1996

So classy and rich, concentrated, proud, individual and fluent.

Cosme Palacio y Hermanos Rioja 1996

Blends an old-style sense of soul with a modern sense of full-frontal fruit.

Enate Tempranillo Cabernet Crianza, Somontano 1995

Gorgeous aromatic fruit of a lovely balance of elements offering richness, texture and a great clinging finish. A classy wine of great style.

Palacio de la Vega Cabernet Sauvignon/ Tempranillo Crianza, Navarra 1995

Wonderful tobaccoey richness and tannins here. Great panache! The texture, the fruit, the sheer energy is terrific.

Palacio de la Vega Merlot, Navarra 1994 `15` `D`

Priorat Blend 24 Garnatxa/Carinyena 1997 `15.5` `C`

Is this an Oddbins speciality? Superripe fruit with lively tannins?

Veganueva Garnacha 1996 `15.5` `C`

Vina Sardana Tempranillo, Catalayud 1996 `16` `C`

Wonderful delicacy of fruit yet it's concentrated and ripe and rich.

Vinas del Vero Cabernet Sauvignon, Somontano 1995 `15` `C`

Vinas del Vero Oak Aged Pinot Noir, Somontano 1995 `13.5` `C`

SPANISH WINE WHITE

Albacora Barrel Fermented Verdejo/ Chardonnay, Vino de Mesa 1996 `14` `D`

Burgans Albarino, Rias Baixas 1997 `13.5` `D`

Very austere as it finishes.

Cosme Palacio y Hermanos Blanco Rioja 1996 `13` `D`

Don't like the ripe finish.

Marino White, Berberana   13.5   B

Vega Sindoa Chardonnay, Navarra 1996   14   D

USA WINE RED

Bonterra Zinfandel, Mendocino 1996   16.5   E

A wonderfully exotic specimen of warmth and immediacy.
Spicy, chewy, softly tannic, hedgerow fruited, it has immense
charm and forwardness.

Fetzer Bonterra Cabernet 1995 (organic)   15   E

Rich, rounded, full, Californian in ripeness and tannic cosiness
from nose to throat.

Fetzer Syrah 1996   16   E

Gives syrah a new dimension of tannic spiciness. Wonderful
richness and ripeness here.

**Fetzer Vineyards Barrel Select Pinot
Noir 1996**   15   E

Really classy pinot which puts many a Volnay at three times the
price to shame.

**Fetzer Vineyards Home Ranch Zinfandel
1996**   14   D

Rich and juicy.

Fetzer Vineyards Pinot Noir 1996 | 15 | D |

Classic stuff – if a touch warmer than normal.

Franciscan Oakville Zinfandel, Napa 1995 | 16 | E |

Very soft yet spiked with lovely gobbets of rich, dry fruit. Nicely mature and superfit.

Franciscan Pinnacles Vineyards Pinot Noir 1997 | 13 | E |

Lovely aroma, pity about the cherryade after.

Lot 21 Marrietta Old Vines, Geyserville NV | 13.5 | E |

Very juicy. Needs a good (mild) curry with it.

Rocking Horse Lamborn Vineyard Zinfandel, Horwell Mountain 1994 | 12 | G |

Fine Wine Stores only.

USA WINE   WHITE

Bonny Doon Framboise (half bottle) | 16 | D |

Wonderful concentrated fruit. Incredible crushed cassis aroma and flavour. Pour it over ice-cream or use it as an aperitif addition to dry white or sparkling wine.

Ca'del Solo Bloody Good White 1997 | 13 | D |

Echo Ridge Fume Blanc 1996 `15.5` `C`

My God! Doesn't it put many Pouillys to shame! Rich yet elegant, interesting smoky edge.

Fetzer Bonterra Chardonnay 1996 `16` `E`

Deliciously classy, rich, controlled and well balanced. A sane reason to spend eight quid on a wine.

Fetzer Vineyards Dry Gewurztraminer, Mendocino 1997 `15.5` `D`

Really dry, gently spicy and fruity without being remotely sweet. An individual specimen of some class.

Fetzer Vineyards Viognier 1997 `15.5` `E`

Lovely fresh apricot and peach wine which sustains its stylishness from nose to throat.

Franciscan Oakville Estate Cuvee Sauvage Chardonnay 1995 `16` `F`

Fed up with puny Puligny? Try this most exuberant and beautifully woody specimen.

Landmark Damaris Chardonnay 1994 `16` `G`

Fine Wine shops only.

Landmark Overlook Chardonnay, 1996 `15` `F`

Elegantly cut, very expensive, chic fruit of class and cuteness.

Mariquita 1994 `13.5` `C`

FORTIFIED WINE

Osbourne Vintage Port 1995
17 G

A truly brilliant texture and richness here. A terrific port for the money. Beats many a more hallowed name for price, pertinency, sheer richness and velvety thickness and great, deep complexity. One of the best young vintage ports I've tasted.

Quinta do Crasto LBV 1991
16 E

One of the best LBVs around. Lovely figgy fruit and velvet texture. Good for several years yet.

SPARKLING WINE/CHAMPAGNE

Champagne Alfred Gratien NV
13 G

Fine Wine Shops only.

Champagne Pommery 1990
14.5 H

Deakin Estate Brut (Australia)
13.5 D

Deutz Marlborough Cuvee (New Zealand)
15 E

Delicious – no other word for it.

Graham Beck Blanc de Blancs (South Africa)
13 E

Gratien & Meyer Saumur Cuvee Flamme Brut NV (France)
12 E

Lindauer Special Reserve (New Zealand) `15.5` `E`

Seaview Brut `14` `D`

Seppelt Great Western Brut (Australia) `13.5` `D`

Still a bargain. Elegant and dry.

Shadow Creek Californian Blanc de Noirs `14.5` `E`

SPAR

LIZ SHOWS HOW A SINGLE WOMAN CAN PUSH
2200 GROCERS AROUND!

Miss Elizabeth Aked runs the wine buying show here and it
can't be any picnic. Indeed, when Eurystheus planned the twelve
labours of Hercules he would, had he known of the position of
wine buyer at Spar, surely have placed it between destroying
the Lernaean Hydra with its hundred heads and mucking out
the stables of Augias where 3000 oxen had been cooped up for
a decade.

Spar shops aren't owned by Spar. The shops are owned by
independent grocers, often just an individual, and so Miss Aked
who has her hands full merely trying to organise her diary to see
suppliers of wine, has also to find the energy to present her little
gems to any willing franchisee.

In spite of these quirks, Spar is something of a success. 1957
to 1997 – last year marked Spar's fortieth anniversary – so they
must be doing something right. (Not necessarily in Scotland.
Looking to raise its profile north of the border, Spar ran a
year-long ad campaign in Scotland featuring, so I was reliably
assured, an Elvis lookalike. Funny year, 1957.)

Spar has been expanding in other areas than kitsch advertising.
Garry Craft, managing director of Spar UK, is on record as
saying the retailer is fighting back hard against the supermarket
giants with initiatives including more top brands, more own
labels, more ready-to-eat hot food, dry cleaning services, in-store
baking and increases in the number of 24-hour stores. Spar also
signed up a deal with Texaco for 29 forecourt stores in Scotland

and agreed to operate 200 stores for the NAAFI at bases in the
UK – said to be worth around £500 million to the retailer over
the next five years. (Does this mean Miss Aked, as a major UK
wine buyer, has had to dress in senior officer's uniform to present
her wares?)

As for the wines, the listing which follows speaks for itself.
Let's hope some of those I-know-my-own-mind Spar grocers
acquire copies of this book so they can appreciate just how well
their wine range could stack up against those supermarkets Mr
Craft wrestles against.

Spar Landmark
32–40 Headstone Drive
Harrow
Middlesex HA3 5QT
Tel: 0181 863 5511
Fax: 0181 863 0603

AUSTRALIAN WINE — RED

Four Winds Red `12` `C`

Hardys Bankside Shiraz 1995 `14` `D`

Lindemans Cawarra Shiraz Cabernet 1996 `14` `C`

AUSTRALIAN WINE — WHITE

Burra Burra Hill Chardonnay 1996 `13.5` `C`

Fat and floppy.

Four Winds White `12` `C`

Lindemans Bin 65 Chardonnay 1996 `15.5` `C`

Lindemans Cawarra Semillon/Riesling 1996 `13.5` `B`

BULGARIAN WINE — RED

Bulgarian Country Red NV `14` `B`

Cheerfully ploughs a tasty plum and strawberry furrow across
the taste buds.

Korten Region Cabernet Sauvignon 1992

BULGARIAN WINE WHITE

Bulgarian Country White NV

A decent warm weather quaffer. Has a muscat-edginess.

CHILEAN WINE RED

Chilean Cabernet Sauvignon 1997

Vigour, richness, balance – it has it all. The fruit is lovely and ripe yet the tannins are rich and velvety. Lovely fruit here.

Chilean Merlot 1997

Leathery, smoky, very dry and gripping. Loads of flavour.

La Fortuna Malbec 1996 15 C

CHILEAN WINE WHITE

Chilean Chardonnay 1997

Curious hint of marzipan tickles the nose and the fruit is lean rather than full. But it's interesting.

Chilean Sauvignon Blanc 1997 | 13.5 | C |

Has some nutty charm.

FRENCH WINE   RED

Claret 1997 | 13.5 | C |

Utterly drinkable. Dry but fruity.

**Cordier Chateau Le Cadet de Martinens,
Margaux 1995** | 14 | E |

Expensive treat. Very plummy and ripe to begin but then the
tannins cruise in and what rich deep tannins they are!

**Corsican Cuvee St Michele Pinot Noir
NV, Spar** | 14 | C |

Not classic pinot and better drunk in Corsica chilled, but a dry
and rustic and warming wine it is.

Coteaux du Languedoc NV | 14 | C |

Excellent value here. Lots of dry, rich fruit with a hint of
rusticity.

Cotes de Ventoux 1995, Spar | 14 | C |

Great country glugging here: warm, dry, herby.

Fitou NV, Spar | 11 | C |

French Country Wine Cabernet Sauvignon/Cinsault NV, Spar (1-litre)

`12.5` **B**

Intimations of herbiness and earthy fruit. A bigger hint would be better. Price bracket has been adjusted to show bottle equivalent.

Gamay VdP du Jardin de la France NV

`12` **C**

Hmm . . .

Gemini Merlot 1996

`13` **C**

Gevrey-Chambertain 1994

`12` **G**

Lot of glum fruit for a lot of dosh. Has some texture and tannins, though.

Hautes Cotes de Beaune 1995

`11` **D**

Lussac St Emilion 1995

`14` **D**

Merlot, VdP d'Oc 1996

`14.5` **B**

Terrific languorousness here: stretches itself fatly and lazily over the taste buds.

Oaked Merlot NV, Spar

`11` **C**

Syrah VdP d'Oc 1996

`13.5` **C**

Juicy yet dry to finish.

VdP de la Cite de Carcassonne Red 1996

`13.5` **B**

Good value. Grippy fruit of some charm.

Vignerons des Pieve, Cuvee San Michele Pinot Noir, Spar   `12` `C`

Vin de Pays de l'Aude Rouge NV   `12` `B`

Cherry simplicity. Very light.

FRENCH WINE   WHITE

Chablis 1996   `10` `E`

Cabbagey and expensive.

French Country Wine NV (1-litre)   `13` `B`

Price bracket has been adjusted to show bottle equivalent.

Gemini Sauvignon Blanc 1997   `14` `C`

A whiplash fruity fish wine: keen, fresh, edgy.

Grenache VdP d'Oc NV, Spar   `14` `B`

Great value glugging here. Simple, dry, fruity without being blowsy.

James Herrick Chardonnay VdP d'Oc 1996   `14` `D`

Always one of the more elegant southern French chardonnays, this vintage has a lemon edge.

Muscadet NV, Spar   `11` `B`

Muscat de St Jean de Minervois (half bottle)   `15` `B`

Oaked Chardonnay NV   `14` `C`

Has warm melon fruit overlording the quiet acidity and this balance makes for a positive finish.

Pouilly Fuisse Les Vercheres 1996   `12` `E`

Rose d'Anjou, Spar   `11` `B`

Sancerre Saget 1996   `10` `D`

Unoaked Chardonnay 1997   `13.5` `C`

Some warmth here.

VdP de la Cite de Carcassonne 1996   `14.5` `B`

Character and bite here, soft to finish yet dry and fruity as it starts off. Brilliant value.

Vin de Pays de l'Aude Blanc NV   `11` `B`

Bit sharp on the tongue.

Vouvray Donatien Bahuaud 1995   `11` `C`

White Burgundy Chardonnay 1996   `11` `D`

GERMAN WINE   WHITE

Grans Fassian Riesling 1995   `14` `D`

I'd lay it down for five or six years. Rate maybe 15/16 then.

HUNGARIAN WINE — RED

Danube Hungarian Country Red, Spar `12` `B`

Misty Mountain Merlot NV, Spar `10` `C`

HUNGARIAN WINE — WHITE

Danube Hungarian Country White, Spar `13` `B`

Misty Mountain Chardonnay, Spar `14` `B`

ITALIAN WINE — RED

Ariento Sangiovese del Rubicone NV `10` `C`

So juicy!

Barolo 'Costa di Bussia' 1994 `13` `F`

Too expensive, I'm afraid. Has some minor typicity but not £13's worth.

Chianti 1997, Spar `14` `C`

Some fatness of fruit plus that baked earthiness. Great pasta plonk.

Chianti Classico Le Fioraie 1995

Expensive juice with tannins.

Montepulciano d'Abruzzo 1997

Great juicy, earthy, cherry/plum fun. Lovely texture.

Pasta Red NV (1-litre)

Bit spineless. Price bracket has been adjusted to show bottle equivalent.

Rondolle Negramaro/Cabernet NV

Infinitely preferable (richer and more robust) to the Pasta Red and more of a bet with pasta.

Sicilian Red Table Wine, Spar 15 B

Valpolicella, Spar 12 B

ITALIAN WINE WHITE

Pasta White NV (1-litre) 14 B

Excellent crispness and delicate fruitiness. Always fresh with its screwcap. Price bracket has been adjusted to show bottle equivalent.

Rondolle Bianco, Spar 10 C

Sicilian White Table Wine, Spar 14.5 B

Soave NV `12.5` `B`

Fairly basic but has suggestions of crispness.

Trebbiano d'Abruzzo 1997 `12.5` `B`

MORAVIAN WINE RED

Moravian Vineyards Czech Red Wine `11` `C`

MORAVIAN WINE WHITE

Moravian Vineyards Czech White Wine `12` `C`

PORTUGUESE WINE RED

Dona Elena Portuguese Red, Spar `13` `B`

Sogrape Vinho de Monte Altenejo 1993 `13` `D`

PORTUGUESE WINE WHITE

Dona Elena Portuguese White, Spar `13.5` `B`

PORTUGUESE WHITE

Vinho Verde NV `10` `C`

SOUTH AFRICAN WINE RED

Longridge Bay View Cabernet Pinotage 1997 `13` `D`

Expensive gushing fruitiness.

Paarl Heights Red 1995 `14.5` `C`

South African Classic Red NV `13` `C`

Very bruised and ripe, this fruit.

Table Mountain Pinot Noir NV `13.5` `C`

Like your average Nuits St Georges. Can't pay it a higher compliment than that.

SOUTH AFRICAN WINE WHITE

Longridge Bay View Chenin Chardonnay 1997 `13.5` `D`

Crisp and fresh.

South African Classic Chardonnay 1997 `14` `C`

Citrussy, vegetal, incisive. Good food wine.

South African Classic White NV `13.5` C

Touch grassy and pear-droppy. Fun slurping – wish it were cheaper, though.

Table Mountain Chenin Blanc `13.5` B

Table Mountain Chenin Blanc 1997 `11` B

SPANISH WINE   RED

Albor Campo Viejo Rioja 1996 `15` C

Campo Rojo Red NV `14` B

Very ripe and juicy yet has back-up tannins providing grip and richness. Needs food. It's too ripe to quaff.

Perfect for Parties Red NV (1-litre) `12` B

One suspects the Parties in mind here are electoral failures. Charming but . . . (Price bracket has been adjusted to show bottle equivalent).

Rioja La Catedral NV `15` C

Lovely tobacco scented plums with a hint of spice – terrific quaffing wine.

Valdepenas NV, Spar `11` B

Juicy . . .

Valencia Soft Red NV `11` B

SPANISH WINE — WHITE

Campo Verde Carinena `14` `B`

Perfect for Parties White NV (1-litre) `10` `B`

I'm sorry, Liz and Alex, but don't invite me to this party. I'm too old. Price bracket has been adjusted to show bottle equivalent.

Valencia Dry White NV `13` `B`

USA WINE — RED

Fetzer Eagle Peak Merlot 1996 `14.5` `D`

Begins quite demurely then provides some real depth.

Fetzer Zinfandel 1995 `14.5` `D`

Very excitingly textured and rich.

Fir Tree Ridge `12.5` `C`

USA WINE — WHITE

Fetzer Sundial Chardonnay 1996 `14.5` `D`

Impressive finesse yet fullness here. Rich and warm yet crisp and beautifully balanced. Has great elegance.

Fir Tree Ridge 13.5 C

FORTIFIED WINE

Old Cellar Fine Ruby Port NV 12 D

Rich and sweet.

Old Cellar LBV Port 1991 11 E

Terribly sweet and simplistic.

SPARKLING WINE/CHAMPAGNE

Marques de Prevel Champagne NV 10 F

Dry and austere. Prefer to drink Cava, thanks.

THRESHER
(+ WINE RACK &
BOTTOMS UP)

HOWSE BAFFLES US WITH BLATHER AS BOOZE
BARN BITES THE DUST!

What a curious retailer we have here. Mr David Howse, its public relations manager, would not be out of place as a character in *Through the Looking Glass*. Who I have in mind here is Humpty Dumpty; not, you understand, as a physical presence but as a philosopher; the Humpty who said 'When I make a word do a lot of work . . . I always pay it extra.' (Mr Howse's best joke was the front cover of the chain's June/July wine list which featured a Thresher shop assistant saying to a customer 'Chateau Giscours? Yes of course sir. Is that the red top, the green top or the gold top sir?' with the word 'allegedly' appended to satisfy the lawyers. Readers may need reminding of the Giscours scandal which broke in early June to the effect that unproven allegations had been levelled in France at this grand cru classe Bordeaux on the grounds that it added illegal substances to its wine – including milk!* – as well as indulged in certain

---

* It must, in all fairness, be pointed out here that milk can justifiably be used in wine production, and I have seen it so employed by a New Zealander, to clarify or fine a wine. Quite what it would do as an additive is not so clear. (Sorry, bad pun, but that's the Howse knock-on effect for you.) As a matter of ironic interest the report in *Le Monde* the day the scandal broke quoted an ex-employee as saying the milk was used to remove 'off odours'. Not half so 'off' those 'odours' as the stink their mode of removal created.

other malpractices which it is not my intention to comment on further at this time.)

But then, that said, Thresher itself bustles with marvellous characters who say things which even a Victorian mathematics don like Lewis Carroll would have found puzzling. When earlier this year Thresher announced that it was to close its pilot Booze Barn outlet at Staples Corner in London, Mr Jerry Walton, Thresher's managing director, said that the project 'had not worked out as we would have liked in terms of the numbers we set ourselves.' Does this mean it didn't make money? Does 'numbers' refer to numbers of customers? It sounds like the cry of the unsuccessful gambler, throwing dice perhaps; whatever it means, it is certainly beyond the ken of the humble wine commentator to understand except to say that Staples Corner, a north London landmark the motorist is very pleased to pass, is a suburban nightmare of such proportions that I can't imagine anything working satisfactorily in its environs except, perhaps, a scrap metal merchant. It's a great pity the numbers didn't work out for Mr Walton. Had they done so we would have seen lots of Booze Barns (dreadful name but there you are, that's Lewis Carroll for you), but since 'there are no further plans' for them as the retailer has also been quoted as saying, I think we can take it that the project is dead and buried beneath the paucity of numbers it failed to reach.

What does this leave us with? It leaves us with a disparate chain of various Thresher outlets from the Thresher Wine Shop,which in my experience* is an uneven enterprise, to the more polished interiors and more knowledgeably staffed Wine Racks and Bottoms Ups. There is no doubt in my mind of the quality of this retailer's wine buying department, staffed as it is with people like the engaging and hugely committed Mr Kim Tidy and the gloriously energetic and vivacious Miss Lucy Warner. But the gap between the buying department's energy and skill and that shown on the shop floor is wide and much greater than that which exists in a comparable set-up like

Oddbins where there is a seamless join between the buyers at HQ and the oily rags in the shops.

If this retailer needs a focus for its operations, it is not one which will come from splintering yet further its retail estate, or mucking about with warehouses. It needs to get the people, *all* the people not just a splendid few in certain branches, who man and woman the counters to be worthy of the trust placed in them by the Tidys and the Warners of this world.

* In my Saturday *Guardian* column earlier this year I wrote of my attempts to buy wine from a Threshers Wine Shop. Thresher, having given up trying to persuade customers to part with £23.99 for a bottle of Vouvray Clos du Bourg 1990, knocked it down to £4.99. Keen to taste so monumental a discount, I telephoned my local Wine Rack and said I'll have a bottle. We had one yesterday, I was told, but it's gone. Next, I telephoned another branch. Oh yes, I was told, we've got eight bottles. I was ecstatic. I rushed off to the shop, borrowing my wife's jalopy since I didn't feel I could entrust eight bottles to my handlebars, only to be told that they couldn't find the wine. The manager, who was absent, would ring me tomorrow. I reserved all eight bottles. When I returned to the store, only four bottles could be found. The shop assistant had bagged the other four, alerted to the bargain. As I controlled my anger at this double-cross, the manager claimed the assistant had misunderstood. The manager rang the assistant, who had already drunk one bottle, and asked for the other three to be returned and a week later, pedalling past, I picked up my seven bottles. The wine was *vaut le detour* but the merry dance I was led was not worthy of a sophisticated wine retailer. It is also to be noted that having written about this incident in my newspaper not a single person at Thresher telephoned me, out of curiosity to ask for more details, or even merely to expostulate along the lines of 'this sort of thing just won't do'.

Thresher
Sefton House
42 Church Road
Welwyn Garden City
Herts AL8 6PJ
Tel: 01707 328244
Fax: 01707 371398

SEE STOP PRESS SECTION AT END OF BOOK FOR LAST-MINUTE ADDITIONS OR UPDATES TO THIS RETAILER'S RANGE.

ARGENTINIAN WINE RED

Corazon Bonarda, Mendoza 1996 `15` `C`

Isla Negra Malbec, Mendoza 1997 `15` `D`

Classic Argentine malbec, it seems to me: juicy and ripe yet dry.

Isla Negra Syrah, Mendoza 1997 `16.5` `D`

More rampant than any Aussie for the same money. Terrific style here.

La Rural Malbec 1996 `15` `C`

Libertad Sangiovese Malbec 1996 `13` `C`

ARGENTINIAN WINE WHITE

**Corazon Chardonnay Chenin, Mendoza
1996** `14` `C`

AUSTRALIAN WINE RED

Apex Grenache/Mourvedre/Shiraz 1996 `13` `E`

Not at Thresher Wine Shops.

Chapel Hill Coonawarra Cabernet Sauvignon 1996 `15.5` `E`

Stylish tannins here and they give the fruit character and backbone.

Chapel Hill Shiraz, McLaren Vale 1996 `14` `E`

Lot of loot for such jammy ripeness... but... there are tannins!!!

Heritage Cabernet Malbec 1995 `13` `E`

Bit soft for a tenner. Hard on the pocket.

Jacobs Creek Shiraz/Cabernet 1996 `14` `D`

Still a wine to reckon with.

Nanya Estate Malbec/Ruby Cabernet 1997 `14` `C`

Drink it chilled with a salad of cos lettuce, garlic (a lot!), green olive oil and sherry vinegar, with fried blood sausage. What an adventure for the palate!

Oxford Landing Estate Black Grenache 1996 `14` `D`

Black cherry richness and dryness.

Penfolds Bin 28 Kalimna Shiraz 1995 `16` `E`

A product of science and deliberation yet none of this is apparent in the rich, dry fruit. Style with guts.

Penfolds Bin 35 Cabernet Sauvignon/ Shiraz/Ruby Cabernet 1996 `15.5` `D`

Rich, layered, clinging, ripe – a great steak and kidney pudding wine.

Red Cliffs Coonawarrra Cabernet Sauvignon 1996

`14.5` `C`

Red Cliffs Reserve Black Label Cabernet Sauvignon 1996

`15.5` `D`

Superbly classy fruit and tannin artefact.

Red Cliffs Shiraz 1997

`16` `C`

Best vintage yet. In its '97 manifestation, it's rich and soupy yet with remarkably well tailored tannins. A terrific wine.

Riddoch Cabernet Shiraz, Coonawarra 1995

`14` `D`

Rich, fleshy, ripe, and with a hint of mint. You may decide to pour it over your lamb chop as well as drinking it with it.

Riddoch 'Limited Release' Coonawarra Shiraz 1996

`15` `D`

Soupy and deep with a hint of tannin which lingers, coating the teeth deliciously.

Rosemount Cabernet Sauvignon, Hunter Valley 1996

`14.5` `E`

Big, juicy, rich.

Rosemount Estate Merlot 1996

`14.5` `E`

Vivid softness to the fruit. Most extraordinary level of texture.

Rosemount Estate Shiraz 1997

`15` `D`

Some weight to the fruit which strikes guilelessly jammy at first, before the tannins cut in.

173

Rosemount Grenache Shiraz 1997 `13.5` `D`

More Aussie juice.

Samuel's Bay Pinot Noir 1997 `13` `D`

Samuel's Bay Malbec, Padthaway 1995 `13` `E`

St Hallett Barossa Shiraz 1995 `14` `E`

Class, precision, richness and calmness.

St Hallett Grenache 1996 `15` `E`

Very classy, dry, rich, vibrant and stylish. Most beautiful balance of acid/fruit/tannin. Good to see such poised structure in an Aussie wine.

Tatachilla Grenache Mataro 1997 `14.5` `C`

Rich, ripe, very ready. A hugely sunny wine of depth and flavour.

Tatachilla Grenache Shiraz, McLaren Vale 1997 `15` `D`

Such energy and softness to the fruit, the unique Aussie trick, gives the wine quaffability and substance.

Tollana Black Label Cabernet Sauvignon 1996 `14` `C`

An excellent food wine. Has a really good acid/fruit balance and grip. Almost European in its structure.

Tollana Dry White 1997 `14` `C`

Dry? *Dry?* Well, I guess it depends on how dry you consider sweet melon acidity to be.

Tollana Red, SE Australia NV | 13.5 | C

AUSTRALIAN WINE WHITE

Amberley Margaret River Semillon 1996 | 13 | E

Not wild about this. Wine Rack and Bottoms Up only.

David Traeger Verdelho, Victoria 1997 | 16 | E

Gorgeous richness here and textured ripeness which makes out a case for verdelho over chardonnay. A very individual wine.

Jacobs Creek Chardonnay 1997 | 15 | C

An excellent ripe, polished texture combined with smoky melon and lemon fruit.

Jacobs Creek Dry Riesling 1997 | 14 | C

A genuinely dryly rich riesling for oriental food.

Katnook Sauvignon Blanc, Coonawarra 1997 | 14 | E

Great aromatic come-on, and terrific gooseberry and grass flavours on the tongue. The finish? Touch and go here.

Lenswood Adelaide Hills Sauvignon Blanc, Tim Knappstein 1997 | 16 | F

Extreme elegance here – like a haut couture creation: hand sewn, silky, beautifully formed and well fitting. Wine Rack only.

Lindemans Bin 65 Chardonnay 1997 `16.5` `C`

Brilliant value: rich, gently spicy (an echo really) to ripe fruit, and a great balance. The '97 is back to being the best under £5 Aussie whites around – or one of them, certainly.

Oxford Landing Estate Viognier 1996 `13` `D`

Oxford Landing Sauvignon Blanc 1997 `14` `C`

Hints of clean classiness.

Penfolds Barossa Valley Semillon Chardonnay 1997 `16.5` `D`

Love its richness and utter regality. It really lords it over other chardonnay blends.

Penfolds Bin 202 Riesling 1997 `15` `C`

A crisp, clean, rather elegant wine for fish dishes where the wok has taken some trouble to prepare.

Pewsey Vale Riesling, Eden Valley 1997 `15.5` `D`

Gorgeous delicacy yet fire-in-its-belly fruitiness which blends fresh and baked fruit, soft and hard, along with steely acidity. A lovely, genuinely fish-friendly wine – and classy. Not at Thresher Wine Shops.

Primo Estate Colombard, Adelaide Plains 1997 `14` `D`

Classy, a trifle expensive, smoky and full. Love to taste it with a Thai mussel soup. Not at Thresher Wine Shops.

Red Cliffs Estate Colombard Chardonnay 1997

`14` `C`

A deep clash of soft richness and pert freshness.

Red Cliffs Sauvignon Blanc 1997

`14` `C`

An excellent fish wine of firmness of purpose and excellent balance.

Riddoch Chardonnay, Coonawarra 1996

`16` `D`

Super mouth-filling plumpness of ripe fruit here, hint of caramel cream even, but the acidity surges alongside in support and the finish is regal. Very classy wine.

Rosemount Estate Chardonnay 1996

`15.5` `D`

Rosemount Estate Diamond Label Chardonnay 1997

`16` `D`

One of the great island's classiest chardonnays – here showing the forwardness of the brilliant '97 vintage.

Rosemount Estate Show Reserve Chardonnay 1996

`15.5` `E`

Gently woody with incisive yet calm and very collected fruit. Sophisticated in feel.

Samuels Bay Colombard 1997

`14` `D`

Rich and almost rumbustious, this has loads of flavour and personality. Do not serve it to anyone over 60. They may not be aware grapes can taste like this. Not at Thresher Wine Shops.

Samuels Bay Riesling, Eden Valley 1997

`16` `D`

Very rich, thick fruit with a touch of exoticism which will be brilliant with oriental food.

177

Samuels Bay Sauvignon Blanc 1997 | 13.5 | D

Good but does it have to cost seven quid?

Samuels Bay Unoaked Chardonnay 1997 | 14 | D

Very richly textured and ripe.

The Willows Vineyard Semillon, Barossa Valley 1995 | 16 | E

It even smells thick! Can texture have an aroma? This wine's can. It's so rich you could weatherproof the average semi from one bottle.

Tim Adams Semillon 1995 | 12 | E

Tollana Black Label Chardonnay 1997 | 14 | C

Nice richness and near-oiliness to the texture on the finish.

Tollana Unoaked Chardonnay 1997 | 15.5 | C

Amazing richness considering it's wood free. Full of verve, vim, style, and ultimate richness, this is a terrific tipple for the money.

Tollana Yellow Label Chardonnay 1997 | 13 | C

BULGARIAN WINE   RED

Iambol Cabernet Sauvignon 1995 | 14 | B

Iambol Special Reserve Cabernet Sauvignon 1993 | 15 | C

Iambol Vintage Blend Cabernet/Merlot, Domaine Boyar 1997   `14` `B`

Vigour and straightforward wine: dry, earthy, plummy.

Plovdiv Cabernet Sauvignon 1993   `15` `B`

Very dry but it has a gentle friskiness – pleasing in what seems a wine in middle-age.

Reserve Cabernet Sauvignon Sliven 1990   `16` `C`

Aroma and fruit begin as dry and richly fruity and a touch exotic then the throat is moved to recognise cedarwood undertones which are reminiscent of an ancient musty Medoc.

Russe Country Red Cabernet/Cinsault NV   `13.5` `B`

Cheap enough and marginally cheerful.

BULGARIAN WINE   WHITE

Chardonnay Reserve Khan Krum 1995   `15` `C`

Interesting vegetal development and maturity. Makes an excellent partner for posh fish dishes.

Targovischte Barrel Fermented Chardonnay 1996   `15` `C`

The poor woman's Puligny? Not a bit of it. The shrewd woman's blue-mood lifter, more like.

Targovischte Chardonnay 1996   `14` `B`

In spite of a 'Cornish Riviera' poster label the fruit is modern, fresh, and very engaging.

CHILEAN WINE   RED

Caballo Loco No 2, Valdivieso NV   `15.5` `F`

Much better than the first release of this wine. The number two
is more elegant and very impactful. Wine Rack only.

Casa Lapostolle Cabernet Sauvignon, Rapel Valley 1996   `16.5` `D`

Superb elegance and tannic richness. Superb, world class wine.

Concha y Toro Casillero del Diablo Cabernet Sauvignon 1996   `16.5` `C`

Deeper, darker, more exotic than previous vintages, this cabernet
is very savoury and rich, subdued tannically, and with a softness
yet solidity of great class.

Cono Sur 20 Barrel Pinot Noir, Rapel Valley 1995   `14` `E`

Errazuriz Cabernet Sauvignon 1996   `16` `C`

Complexity under a fiver is rare enough. Texture uncommon.

Errazuriz Cabernet Sauvignon Reserva 1995   `16.5` `E`

Tobacco and a warm saddle – so a lonesome cowboy makes the
first impression – but the pace of the fruit and finish make for
a long-drawn-out death of moving sublimity.

Isla Negra Cabernet Sauvignon, Rapel Valley 1996   `15` `C`

How is it possible to conjure texture like this from grapes?

Compellingly soft and attractive – on all fronts (and as far as the tongue is concerned, back and sides also).

Las Colinas Cabernet Sauvignon 1997 `15.5` `C`

Superb soft texture without soppiness. Rich and fulfilling.

Las Colinas Chilean Red 1997 `15` `B`

The woman of taste's every day quaffing red. Live happy on a bottle a day.

Las Colinas Merlot, Curico Valley 1997 `15` `C`

How to combine muscularity with litheness. Strength with delicacy.

Santa Ines Legado de Armida Reserve Carmenere, Maipo Valley 1996 `14.5` `D`

Delicious texture and ripe fruit, improving nicely in bottle. Makes a real case out for itself, richly and softly, with a lovely dry finish. Not at Thresher Wine Shops.

Santa Ines Legardo de Armida Reserve Cabernet Sauvignon 1997 `16` `D`

Very chocolatey, rich and dry, great tannins.

Santa Ines Legardo de Armida Reserve Malbec 1997 `16` `D`

Rich, gentle and powerful, very dry and lingering. Wine Rack and Bottoms Up only.

Santa Ines Legardo de Armida Reserve Merlot 1997 `17` `D`

Fantastic coffee tannins and rich, complex fruit. Wonderful texture and richness. Wine Rack and Bottoms Up only.

Trio Merlot 1996

New leather, soft fruit, tannin, and a finish combining Earl Grey tea, coffee and ripe soft damson and blackberries. An awesomely delicious wine for the money.

Valdivieso Cabernet Sauvignon 1997 16.5 C

Fantastic lingering fruit which offers a double whammy on the finish – a secondary explosion of flavour as it descends.

Valdivieso Cabernet Sauvignon Reserve 1996 15 D

Vibrant richness, tonality and a good dry finish. Not at Thresher Wine Shops.

Valdivieso Malbec 1997 16 C

Such rich charms on display here. The controlled exuberance of the fruit is a marvel to quaff. Not at Thresher Wine Shops.

Valdivieso Merlot, Lontue 1997

Gorgeous texture for such youth! Deep, rich, softly leathery, aromatic and bold. Selected stores.

Wine Rack 'Own Label' Merlot/Cabernet, Maipo 1995

CHILEAN WINE WHITE

35 Sur Sauvignon Blanc, Lontue Valley 1997 15 C

Grassy richness and deep texture here. Terrific shellfish wine.

Casa Lapostolle Sauvignon Blanc 1997 `16` `C`

Cono Sur Gewurztraminer 1997 `15` `C`

Dry, hint of spice, fresh, gushing yet restrained. Delicious.

Errazuriz 'La Escutura Estate' Chardonnay, Casablanca Valley 1996 `16` `D`

Very elegant and richly flavoured by the sun of Chile. It brightens up your day in one sip.

Isla Negra Chardonnay, Casablanca 1997 `14.5` `D`

Uncommonly crisp and nutty for a Chilean chardonnay. But very neatly turned out, if somewhat lean rather than plump.

Las Colinas Sauvignon Blanc 1997 `14.5` `C`

Chile takes sauvignon and turns it into something so deliciously alien and alert! X-files stuff! Unexpected and pacey.

Santa Carolina Cabernet Rose 1997 `15` `C`

One of the more delicious examples of a slightly despised breed, the winter rose. Charming manners and disposition.

Santa Carolina Sauvignon Blanc Nouveau 1997 `15` `C`

Fresh as the morning dew and will lose its charms almost as quickly. A delicious, all-round glug.

Santa Ines Legardo de Armida Reserve Chardonnay 1997 `17.5` `D`

Such vast richness of tone, elegance and sheer gorgeous texture – a world class wine at an absurd price. Wine Rack and Bottoms Up only.

Santa Rita Reserva Chardonnay, Maipo Valley 1995

One of those wines which brings instant elevation to the black mood you returned home with. One sip of this wonderfully rich, soft, invigorating, fresh, hugely quaffable, immensely classy, utterly ambrosial stuff – and you're floating. Not at Thresher Wine Shops.

Soleca Semillon, Colchagua Valley 1997

Fabulously rich fruit here: ripe melon, raspberries, limes and pineapples. And it has a plastic, taint-free cork!

Trio Chardonnay, Concha y Toro 1996

Has lemon and slight pear undertones moving gently under the rich, positively charged fluid. Very stylish.

Wine Rack 'Own Label' Chilean Chardonnay 1997

Bit foppish on the finish.

FRENCH WINE RED

Andre Lurton Oak-aged Claret 1994

13 D

Big Frank's Best Red Shiraz d'Oc 1996

15.5 D

Bright, rich, red, throat-soothing fruit.

Chateau Bonnet Rouge, Bordeaux 1995

Chateau Cap de Faugeres, Cotes de Castillon 1993 | 15.5 | E

Superb dry and classic richness of attack. Terrific character and style.

Chateau Coucheroy Pessac-Leognan, Graves 1995 | 13 | D

Rather too soft.

Chateau Mercier Cotes de Bourg 1996 | 14.5 | D

Lovely plump texture. Most unusual in a Bordeaux at this price.

Chateau Puy Bardens, 1er Cotes de Bordeaux 1996 | 13.5 | C

Chateau Puy Bardens Cuvee Prestige, 1er Cotes de Bordeaux 1996 | 12.5 | E

Chateau Rose d'Orion Montagne, St Emilion 1996 | 14.5 | D

Lovely blackcurrant dryness. Clinging finish of some wit.

Chateau Suau, 1er Cotes de Bordeaux 1996 (unoaked) | 13 | C

Chateauneuf-du-Pape Les Oliviers 1997 | 11 | E

Claret Regional Classic, Sichel NV | 14 | C

Old-fashioned claret dryness and earthiness.

Cotes de Ventoux La Mission 1996 | 13 | B

Cotes du Rhone Chateau du Grand Prebois 1995
13.5 | D

Cotes du Rhone Villages Vinsorbes, Domaine de la Bicarelle 1995
15.5 | E

So warm and gently spicy, tannic and fruity, it works by stealth and guile, not by muscle and sheer power. A real sippin' red. Wine Rack only.

Domaine de Martialis St Emilion 1994
13.5 | F

Not at Thresher Wine Shops.

Domaine de Montine, Coteaux du Tricastin 1995
13.5 | C

L'Esprit de Chevalier, Pessac Leognan 1994
13.5 | G

Not at Thresher Wine Shops.

La Demoiselle de Sociando, Haut Medoc 1995
13.5 | F

Not at Thresher Wine Shops.

Les Allees de Cantemerle, Haut Medoc 1995
13 | E

Mas de Daumes Gassac 1993
14 | E

Merlot Bordeaux, Lurton 1996
13 | C

Minervois Domaine Ste Eulalie 1995
14.5 | C

Rustic charmer with some sweet plum fruit to its brisk earthiness.

Morgon Duboeuf 1997 `13` `D`

Lot of money – touch of baloney.

Moulin-a-Vent Domaine de la Tour de Bief 1996 `12` `E`

Oak Aged Cotes du Rhone, Gabrielle Meffre 1997 `15.5` `C`

Delicious earthy fruit. Classy, modern/ancient, ripe, dry, warm and welcoming.

Regional Classics Beaujolais 1996 `12` `C`

Second de Durfort, Margaux 1994 `13` `E`

Terroire de Tuchan Fitou 1994 `15.5` `E`

Better, richer, more attractively fruity than many a claret to which it can be compared.

Torgan Valley 'Old Vines' Carignan, VdP du Torgan 1996 `14` `B`

FRENCH WINE WHITE

Chablis 1er Cru Fourchaume, Chateau de Maligny 1995 `16` `F`

Very expensive, but very impressive. It is classic, rich, deep, complex, extremely drinkable and a credit to pricey white burgundy.

Chablis Vieilles Vignes Domaine Daniel Defaix 1996 — 14 E

A lot of dosh for such seemingly austere chardonnay but the finesse on the finish is something worth paying for.

Chateau Bonnet Entre Deux Mers 1997 — 16 D

What a wonderful turn up for the book! This Bordeaux blanc is wonderfully crisp and full of hard fruit flavours and it's topped with vigorous mineralised acids. A truly outstanding shellfish wine. Real class.

Clos de la Fine Muscadet Sur Lie, Cotes de Grandlieu 1997 — 14 C

Rated on the basis that it is drunk with moules marinieres.

Domaine de Tariquet Sauvignon Blanc VdP des Cotes de Gascogne 1996 — 15 C

One of the most elegant Gascons around. Delightful fruit.

Domaine Laroche Chardonnay 'Tete de Cuvee' 1996 — 14 D

Again, France shows us meagre fruit but exciting acids.

Fat Bastard Chardonnay VdP d'Oc 1997 — 15 D

Still fat, still a bastard, still worth keeping nine or twelve months before unloading the fruit (though it's drinkable now).

Garden Valley Chardonnay, VdP du Jardin de la France 1997 — 15 C

Lushness yet not simpering with love-me-please-do fruit – it's a real charmer.

'Garden Valley' Chenin, VdP du Jardin de la France 1996

`14.5` `C`

Fresh, clean, almost clinical – but terrific with shellfish.

Gewurztraminer Turckheim 1997

`16` `D`

Gorgeous richness yet dry peach/melon flavours. Hint of spice, hint of pebbly acidity, hint of crisp vegetality – a lot of hints making great impact.

James Herrick Chardonnay VdP d'Oc 1996

`15` `C`

Good age for a wine not designed to grow old with any great grace. Here it's perfectly mature, melony and lemony and strikes home with style.

Laperouse VdP d'Oc White 1995

`15` `C`

Pinot Blanc Turckheim 1997

`14` `C`

Genuine pinot blanc, vegetal, ripe, steely, crisp and delicious!

Pinot Blanc Zind Humbrecht 1994

`14.5` `E`

Riesling Gueberschwihr Zind Humbrecht 1994

`12` `F`

River Hill Blanc de Blancs Dry, Donatien Bahuaud 1997

`15` `B`

Delicious, firm and crisp and great with fish.

River Hill Blanc de Blancs Medium Dry, Donatien Bahuaud 1997

`12` `B`

Bit dull, adding sugar . . .

Sancerre La Cresle de la Porte 1997 `13.5` `E`

Almost steely, almost gooseberryish, almost fresh and fine . . .
Eight quid for an almost is not good value.

Soleil d'Or Chardonnay VdP Isle de Beaute 1996 `13` `C`

Tokay Pinot Gris, Turckheim 1997 `15` `D`

Hard and rich, apricotiness is delicious and subtle, great
acid/fruit balance. Will develop extremely well for two or
three years.

Vouvray Didier Champalou 1997 `14` `D`

Keep it for five years before opening it. It'll be even richer. Wine
Rack only.

WR/001/96 Chardonnay VdP d'Oc 1996 `16` `D`

Deliciously playful, lemonic and elegantly fruity. Preferable to
any number of Meursaults at five times the price. Wine Rack
stores only.

GERMAN WINE WHITE

Bereich Bernkastel, Regional Classics 1996 `12` `C`

Bereich Nierstein, Regional Classics 1996 `13` `C`

Hock, Regional Classics `10` `B`

Kendermann Riesling Dry 1996 `13` `C`

Piesporter Michelsberg QbA 1997 `10` `B`

Dreadful old-fashioned half-sweet soppiness here.

Solus 1996 `13.5` `C`

This has many virtues, some faults. In this respect it is like all of us. I think the bright blue bottle will appeal to grans, as might the fruit. I would not eschew a glass, chilled, in warm weather.

HUNGARIAN WINE RED

Butlers Blend Hungarian Kekfrancos/ Merlot 1997 `14` `B`

Simple, dry, earthy – with a touch of cheek.

HUNGARIAN WINE WHITE

AK 28 Hungarian Sauvignon Blanc 1997 `15.5` `C`

Superb sauvignon of crispness and class.

AK 68 Hungarian Pinot Gris 1997 `15.5` `C`

A rose of great charm and richness. It works as a great quaffer and a food wine.

Butlers Blend Hungarian Country Wine   `13.5` **B**

Chardonnay Gyongyos 1996   `14` **C**

Sour-faced, true, but is has echoes of chardonnay plumpness
to it. An anorexic chardonnay? Possibly, but one which has its
uses: smoked salmon, tuna salad, winkle pie.

Cool Ridge Barrel Fermented Chardonnay 1995   `13.5` **C**

Bit off-hand for a fiver.

Sauvignon Blanc Gyongyos 1996   `15` **C**

Oyster friendly wine with hints of raw grass. Great price for
such a well-cut, well-rolled lawn.

ITALIAN WINE   RED

Barolo Ceretto 'Zonchera' 1992   `13` **G**

Caramia Negroamaro del Salento 1996   `14` **D**

Elegance with a flash of exuberance on the finish. Not at
Thresher Wine Shops.

Chianti Classico Riserva Ricasoli 1994   `14` **E**

Very ripe and earthy, cherryish and unusually fresh. Not at
Thresher Wine Shops.

La Gioiosa Merlot, Veneto 1997   `14` **C**

Very dry and dapper.

Le Trulle Primitivo del Salento 1996   13.5   C

Morellino di Scansano, Cecchi 1996   15   D

Very ripe, cherry rich and gently baked (but not half). Wine Rack only.

Original Z Primitivo Salente, Cantele 1996   13   C

Primitivo del Salento, Caramia 1996   14.5   D

Lovely richness here, with a deft intermarrying of ripeness with earthy tannicity. Not at Thresher Wine Shops.

Ricasoli Sangiovese Formulae 1995   13.5   E

Ripassa, Valpolicella Classico, Zenato 1994   17   E

The smell of baked fruit, ginger, figs, and ripe raisins. A brilliant Valpolicella made in the old-fashioned Ripassa way, and it's rich and gorgeous. Brilliant with food. Not at Thresher Wine Shops.

Rosso di Puglia Campione   13.5   C

Sangiovese di Toscana, Cecchi 1996   14   C

Wonderful lightness of tone but rich dryness of finish. A terrific little tipple.

'Teuzzo' Chianti Classico Riserva 1995   14   E

Very earthy cherries here. Not at Thresher Wine Shops.

The Sicilian Nero d'Avola Merlot 1997   15   C

Brilliant richness and ripeness here plus warmth of texture.

Valpolicella Classico Superiore, Zenato 1995

Delicious cherry/plum fruit here!

Vino Nobile di Montepulciano Riserva Avignonesi 1993

Lovely lingering earthiness which coats a medley of soft fruits. Wine Rack only.

ITALIAN WINE WHITE

Four Seasons Estate – Summer, Sauvignon NV

Great texture, richness yet crispness.

La Gioiosa Chardonnay, Veneto 1997

Very very dry and confident of itself: Needs food.

Lugana San Benedetto, Zenato 1996

Soft yet dry, delicious with smoked fish. Not at Thresher Wine Shops.

Marche Trebbiano, Moncaro 1997

Well, it would certainly perform decently with squid dishes.

Original 'S' Chardonnay del Salento 1996

Pinot Grigio Fiordaliso Vino da Tavola 1997 　14　 C

Pinot like this, in neatly manicured Italian hands, is crisp and nutty and made for food.

Planeta Chardonnay 1996 (Sicily) 　15.5　 F

£13 for a Sicilian wine? Yep. But if you like woody Meursault in a cool year, then this wine is a treat. Style, class, richness yet finesse (in a sour sort of way).

Soave Classico Superiore, Pieropan 1995 　14　 E

The Sicilian Inzolia Chardonnay 1997 　15.5　 C

Gorgeous richness and nuttiness here. Has a kind of Brazil nut edge to the soft, ripe fruit. An unusual chardonnay.

NEW ZEALAND WINE RED

Church Road Cabernet Sauvignon/Merlot 1995 　16　 E

Got something for the money. Coffee, tea, cassis, leather, texture and tannin. Who minds nine quid when you come back with a complete spice cabinet?

Linden Estate Merlot, Esk Valley, Hawkes Bay 1996 　13　 E

Curiously pinot noir tone to the merlot. Not at Thresher Wine Shops.

Martinborough Vineyard Pinot Noir 1996 　12　 F

Not at Thresher Wine Shops.

Montana Cabernet Sauvignon/Merlot 1995 `14.5` `D`

Palliser Estate Pinot Noir 1996 `14.5` `F`

Expensive treat for pinot lovers. Has classic compost heap ripeness growing in which are wild raspberries and dead game.

NEW ZEALAND WINE WHITE

Azure Bay Medium Dry 1997 `12` `C`

Falls between two stools: is it dry or sweetish? Fails to convince either way.

Azure Bay Sauvignon Blanc/Semillon 1997 `15` `C`

Can't deny the loveliness of the soul (fruit) but why does the suit (the blue bottle and label) have to be so kitsch? Oh well, just call me old-fashioned.

Church Road Reserve Chardonnay, Hawkes Bay 1995 `15` `F`

An expensive treat with a soft, woody/vanilla edge to the fruit. An immensely compelling wine – as long as twelve quid doesn't lose you any sleep. Not at Thresher Wine Shops.

Cooks Gisborne Chardonnay 1997 `13` `D`

Corbans Private Reserve Chardonnay, Gisborne 1995 `16` `E`

It's the creamy integration of wood and fruit, which lingers on the taste buds most deliciously, which give the wine its considerable finesse (yet richness). Not at Thresher Wine Shops.

Hunter's Oak Aged Sauvignon Blanc, Marlborough 1996

| 14 | F |

Very elegant and insouciant. Not at Thresher Wine Shops.

Kapua Springs Medium Dry White, Hawkes Bay 1997

| 12 | C |

Ho-hum indecision here.

Montana Chardonnay, Marlborough 1997

| 14.5 | D |

Crisp and well-finished, nothing herbaceous or overly vegetal. An excellent fish wine.

Montana Reserve Gewurztraminer, Gisborne 1997

| 15.5 | E |

Brilliant finish to the wine completes the job already well worked by the gentle, spicy aroma and the soft fruit. A superb alternative to chardonnay (and much else). Lovely now but will get even lovelier.

Montana Reserve Sauvignon Blanc, Marlborough 1996

| 16 | E |

Oozes class from every drop. Has an underlying, controlled richness of great charm.

Montana Sauvignon Blanc 1997

| 15 | D |

Classy cut of grass – smooth as the lawn on a croquet pitch. But it isn't grotesquely herbaceous whatsoever.

Nobilo White Cloud Muller-Thurgau/ Sauvignon Blanc 1997

| 10 | C |

Amongst the dullest Kiwis I've encountered.

Orchid Vale Medium Chardonnay 1997 · 14.5 · C

Blue bottle, avian label, dotty fruit – it's worth the price of admission just to see the thing on the dinner table.

Ormond Estate Chardonnay 1995 · 13 · E

Palliser Estate Chardonnay 1995 · 15.5 · E

Palliser Estate Sauvignon Blanc 1997 · 15 · E

Very classy with delightful hints of rich grass. An expensive treat.

Stoneleigh Riesling, Marlborough 1996 · 16.5 · C

Staggeringly good! Great classic riesling smell, fruit . . . and finish? Ah well . . . the finish is in a different class altogether. It's quite quite delicious. A gorgeous wine. To be drunk young.

Te Kairanga Barrel Aged Sauvignon Blanc 1996 · 14 · E

Clean and fresh, with undoubted charm and improving quite well in bottle, but at over nine quid it lacks complexity. Not at Thresher Wine Shops.

Timara Medium Dry Chardonnay/Semillon, Montana 1996 · 14 · C

Now the medium works. The fruit is not sweet, the acid is in good fettle.

Villa Maria Lightly Oaked Chardonnay, Marlborough 1996 · 14 · D

A little more oak might be better. So would a little more fruit. But the grapes do sing for their supper (melodiously so if chicken's on the plate).

Villa Maria Riesling 1997 | 14 | C

Good impact and some rich, clean fruit on the taste buds – perhaps a bit limp on the finish. But still rates well.

Villa Maria Sauvignon Blanc 1997 | 16.5 | D

Back to form! A superbly classy sauvignon with hints of gunsmoke and ripe melon, with lovely, balanced acidity, gently grassy but more importantly minerally.

PORTUGUESE WINE   RED

Alandra Esporao 1997 | 12 | C

Bright Brothers Douro Red 1996 | 16 | C

Real energy and richness here, modern and full yet also very dry and characterful.

Espiga Red, Estremadura 1997 | 12 | B

Very juicy and ripe.

Esporao Cabernet Sauvignon 1996 | 14 | D

Has some lingering softness to it.

Fiuza Cabernet Sauvignon, Bright Brothers 1995 | 15.5 | C

Delicious hedgerow fruit with a hint of refined earth.

Monte Velho Red 1996 | 13.5 | C

Has some hints of tobacco to it.

SOUTH AFRICAN WINE — RED

Bellingham Pinotage, Franschoek 1997 | 15.5 | D

Classy richness and pinotage pliant fruitiness. Real quaffing wine.

Delheim Cabernet Sauvignon 1994 | 14 | D

Delheim Pinotage 1995 | 14 | D

KWV Cabernet Sauvignon 1996 | 15 | C

Quaffing cabernet with a touch of attitude.

KWV Pinotage 1996 | 16 | C

The essence of juicy pinotage: rich, vibrant, jammy, rubbery, very deep and joyous. Great stuff.

KWV Roodeberg, Coastal Region 1996 | 14 | C

Needs food, for the ripeness finishes dry and food stretches the fruit.

Signature Cinsaut 1997 | 16 | C

Such engaging warmth and richness and soft texture you wonder if it has a real hearth but it strikes cinder-hot and spicy on the finish. Wine Rack stores only.

Villiera Merlot, Paarl 1995 | 14 | E

Touch expensive but it does deliver some stylish fruit especially with the lingering finish.

Winelands Cabernet Sauvignon/Franc, Stellenbosch 1997 | 13.5 | D

Very soft and jammy.

SOUTH AFRICAN WINE · WHITE

Arniston Bay Chenin/Chardonnay 1997 | 15 | C

Cheerful marriage of often glum companions makes a cosy relationship of nuttiness and creaminess, yet crispness.

Bellingham Sauvignon, Franschoek 1996 | 13.5 | C

'Deetlefs' Chardonnay 1997 | 15 | D

Emphatically modern and full of fruit without going gooey on the finish.

'Deetlefs' Chenin Blanc 1997 | 15.5 | D

Immensely stylish chenin which manages to pull off that difficult trick of being clean without being tart, fruity without appearing full. Great poise here.

'Deetlefs' Semillon 1997 | 13.5 | E

Pricey for the simplicity of the style.

Delaire Sauvignon Blanc 1997 | 15 | E

Uniquely expressive of clean gooseberry fruit. A classic sauvignon which owes more to great Sancerre than Marlborough. Wine Rack only.

Delheim Chardonnay 1996 `13` `D`

Delheim 'New Release' Chenin Blanc, Stellenbosch 1996 `15.5` `D`

Halves to Hogsheads Chapter Four Wooded Chenin 1997 `14.5` `C`

Less wood than real crisp, fresh fruit. Deeply delicious and thirst quenching. Wine Rack only.

Hartenberg 'Occasional' Auxerrois 1997 `16` `D`

Tremendous flavour and style here. A quirkily rich, chardonnay-style wine of complexity and real lengthy flavour. A thought-provokingly fruity wine. Not at Thresher Wine Shops.

Hartenberg 'Occasional' Bush Vine Chenin Blanc 1997 `15.5` `D`

Chenin as a class act, almost in the fine Chablis mould. Not at Thresher Wine Shops.

Hartenberg 'Occasional' Pinot Blanc 1997 `15.5` `D`

The flavour comes on coy and demure but then the crisp nutty fruit strikes on the back palate to lift the wine into the high class league. Not at Thresher Wine Shops.

Hartenberg 'Occasional' Semillon 1997 `16` `D`

Vigour, vim, veracity, virtue – it offers the gamut of princely charms and offers them in a flood of controlled, well-refined richness and depth. Balanced, bonny wine. Not at Thresher Wine Shops.

Hartenberg Weisser Riesling, Stellenbosch 1997
13 D

An oddity. Might suit Thai food.

KWV Chenin Blanc 1997
15 C

Gorgeous softness and richness of fruit but it never gets over-whelming or silly. Utterly drinkable.

KWV Sauvignon Blanc 1997
13 C

Very cosmetic edge to the wine.

Millbrook Chenin Blanc 1997
16 C

Brilliant creamy richness, almost like raspberry yoghurt, but the pineapple acidity blends in perfectly. A lovely wine.

Signal Hill Barrel Fermented Chenin 1997
16 C

Brilliant vanillary fruit, woody, gently rich, food friendly and imbued with great charm. Real style here.

'The Collection' Chenin Blanc, Bellingham 1997
15.5 C

Very classy, very modern, razor-sharp fruit of incisiveness and style.

'The Collection' Semillon, Bellingham 1997
15.5 C

Nicely mature in spite of its youth. Very calm, collected, dry and purposeful. Wine Rack only.

Villiera Blanc Fume, Paarl 1997
13.5 D

Rather calm and feet-dragging and finishes with a lack of positiveness.

Villiera Chardonnay 1997   16   E

Delicious vanilla edges to the smoky fruit. A really terrific partner for posh fish like scallop in cream sauce.

Villiera Chenin Blanc 1997   15   C

Just as you think it's a simple crisp young thing it turns rich and tasty and shows great finishing power.

Villiera Gewurztraminer 1996   15   D

Villiera Sauvignon Blanc, Paarl 1997   15   D

Odd sort of texture, plump yet nutty (so it's got a delicious hard-soft tension).

Winelands Early Release Chenin Blanc 1998   14   C

Delicious freshness and fruitiness. Charm without being either soppy or stern.

SPANISH WINE   RED

Agramont Merlot Tempranillo, Navarra 1996   14.5   C

Dry, touch sour on the plummy finish, but essentially very dry and forceful.

Baron de Ley Rioja Reserva 1994   14   D

Touch pricey for dryness but good with food.

Campo Viejo Rioja Reserva 1993 `13` `D`

Casa Rural Red NV `14.5` `B`

A soft fruity red of consummate drinkability. Great price.

Conde de Valdemar Rioja Crianza 1995 `13.5` `D`

Goes a bit gooey as it finishes.

Conde de Valdemar Rioja Reserva 1993 `13` `E`

Copa Real PlataTinto NV `15` `C`

Grippy earthy tannins provide a great backbone to the rich fruit.

Cune Rioja 1995 `13.5` `D`

A little expensive for the simplicity of the style. Bottoms Up only.

Dominio de Valdepusa Cabernet Sauvignon, Marques de Grinon 1996 `16` `E`

Hugely classy beast with flavour, depth, tannins and great purpose. Brilliant bouncy fruit.

Don Darias `14` `B`

Finca Dofi Priorat 1994 `18` `H`

Fabulous rich and well-flavoured specimen of well-deep fruit, brisk tannins, and acidity of the class which suggests the wine will be as good but much softer in ten years. Licorice, figs, chocolate, coffee. Bottoms Up only.

Marques de Grinon Reserva Rioja 1993 `14` `E`

Hmm . . . not sure I like its proximity to eight quid . . .

Martinez Bujanda Rioja Gran Reserva 1990   15   F

Ochoa Reserva 1990   14   E

Only just making this rating (on account of its utter drinkability and charm) but nine quid is a lot for a wine of soft vanilla fruit and calm finish. Bottoms Up only.

Ochoa Tempranillo Crianza 1995   16.5   D

Gorgeous ripeness, fatness, richness yet with it all there is Ochoa's great elegance, smoothness and beautiful tannic cosiness. On the delicate side for all this. Not for robust food. Lovely stuff. Bottoms Up only.

Priorat Les Terrasses 1993   13   G

Loaded with fruit with a chewy edge of textured tannicity. Not as formidable (or as alcoholic) as priorats legendarily are. This one is rich, not too ripe, dry but fat, and voluptuous. Is it worth £18? Hummm . . . Too ripe. Bottoms Up only.

Remonte Cabernet Sauvignon Crianza, Navarra 1995   15   C

Classy ripeness, dry to finish, and plenty of gusto aboard the fruit.

Rioja Torre de Montalbo 1996   13   D

Not quite an over-a-fiver pick of fruit.

Santara Dry Red, Conca de Barbera 1996   15   B

Has some nice characterful tannins sprinkled on top of the fruit.

Scraping the Barrel Tempranillo NV   14   C

Great fun amongst the scrapings here.

Torres Sangre de Toro 1996 `17` `C`

Fantastic vintage for this old warhorse. No bull! This is classy, rich, dry, complex, polished, characterful and very very stylish. It has texture and ripeness. Rich and riveting.

Valdemar Tinto, Rioja 1997 `15.5` `C`

Lush and ripe, very plummy and rich. Lovely texture.

Valencia Red `13` `B`

Vina Albali, Valdepenas Reserva 1991 `15` `C`

Soft, ripe, rich, touch of soil about the finish. A good food red.

Vina Marcos Navarra Tempranillo 1996 `15.5` `C`

Rich and dry, with loads of berried (but not buried) flavours. It is great value for food or mood – good enough for a Christmas day feast.

Vina Real Rioja 1994 `13.5` `D`

Juicy, expensive. Bottoms Up only.

SPANISH WINE WHITE

Albarino Condes del Alberei 1995 `15` `D`

One of the better and more enterprising albarinos. It has class and complexity yet has the texture to be gluggable. It will work wonderfully with food.

Copa Real Blanco NV

An austere, dry, very shellfishy white which shrugs its shoulders and says 'Take it or leave it, that's the way I am.'

Moscatel de Valencia NV

A superbly sticky sweet wine with a honeyed edge. Great with fresh fruit and Christmas cake.

Santara Viura/Chardonnay, Conca de Barbera 1996

Fresh, vividly so in fact, but the hint of underripe hard fruit gives it bite and backbone. Certainly a terrific wine for fish.

Torres Vina Sol 1997

Good solid fruit of some depth which will develop more perfume and complexity over the next year.

USA WINE RED

Byron Pinot Noir, Santa Barbara County 1995

Very sulphurous. Available through Wine Rack Direct.

Columbia Crest Cote de Columbia Grenache 1995

Dunnewood Dry Silk Cabernet, Seven Archers Vineyard, Alexander Valley 1994

Very classy and ripe. And indeed like crumpled silk on the tongue. Not at Thresher Wine Shops.

Dunnewood North Coast Cellars Cabernet 1995

14 D

Fetzer Eagle Peak Merlot 1995

15 D

Soupy and all-embracing.

Fetzer Valley Oaks Cabernet Sauvignon 1995

15.5 D

So approachable and soft.

Fetzer Zinfandel 1995

14.5 D

Very excitingly textured and rich.

Gallo Turning Leaf Cabernet Sauvignon 1995

15 D

Very approachable, soft, ripe, and in the Aussie mould.

Gallo Turning Leaf Zinfandel 1995

13.5 D

Juicy with a hint of earthy wild strawberry.

Redwood Trail Pinot Noir 1996

14.5 D

Excellent, if slightly sulphurous, on first opening, but the texture and ripeness and sheer class of pinot are obvious.

Robert Mondavi North Coast Cellars Zinfandel 1995

15 E

Rich and fresh. Not at Thresher Wine Shops.

Robert Mondavi Oakville District Cabernet 1995

17 H

Hugely expensive but then it is utterly superb: textured, structured, exuberant yet dry, classy and very complex. Available through Wine Rack Direct.

Robert Mondavi Reserve Pinot Noir 1995

Bit sulphurous. Available through Wine Rack Direct.

Saintsbury Pinot Noir, Carneros 1996

Very beautifully textured. Available through Wine Rack Direct.

Sebastiani Old Vines Zinfandel, Sonoma County 1995

Talus Zinfandel, Woodbridge 1995

Vendange Californian Red 1996

Soft and fruity – not a lot more to be said except it has that inexpressibly Californian warmth of texture.

Woodbridge Californian Zinfandel, Robert Mondavi 1995

USA WINE WHITE

Fetzer Sundial Chardonnay, Mendocino County 1997

Resounds with limey, melon-rich fruit.

Fetzer Viognier, Mendocino County 1997

Rich apricot fruit – terrific! And it will age superbly.

Gallo Turning Leaf Chardonnay 1995

Bit obvious (almost tarty) on the finish, but a good price to pay for a partner for smoked eels with horseradish.

Jekel Chardonnay, Gravelstone Vineyards, Monterey County 1996   `16` `D`

The essence of affordable, high class California cool. A chardonnay of ambition, elegance and controlled ripeness.

Kendall Jackson Vintners Reserve Chardonnay 1996   `13` `E`

Kendall Jackson wines are a sad reflection on a once first class label. Not at Thresher Wine Shops.

Robert Mondavi Carneros Unfiltered Chardonnay 1995   `13` `G`

Too expensive, if far from undrinkable. Not at Thresher Wine Shops.

Robert Mondavi Fume Blanc, Napa Valley 1995   `14` `F`

Deliciously crisp and vivid – touch pricey for these privileges, though. Available through Wine Rack Direct.

St Supery Dollarhide Ranch Sauvignon Blanc, Napa Valley 1997   `16` `E`

Very forward, rich, toffee-textured and lingering. Lovely wine for complex fish dishes.

Vendange Californian Dry White 1996   `14` `C`

Curiously delicious oriental pear (ripe) fruit.

Wente Riva Ranch Reserve Chardonnay 1995   `16` `E`

Chewy richness, spiced melon, wood, vanilla and lemon. Gorgeous. Not at Bottoms Up.

**Woodbridge Californian Sauvignon Blanc,
Robert Mondavi 1996** 13 D

Gently sticky and oddly ripe and rather expensive.

SPARKLING WINE/CHAMPAGNE

Angas Brut 16 D

Simply great value for money: stylish, subtly fruity, classically
dry yet not austere.

Angas Brut Rose (Australia) 15.5 D

Asti Martini (Italy) 10 D

Castelblanch Cava Extra Brut 13 C

Charles Heidsieck 'Mis en Cave 1992' NV 13 H

Bottoms Up only.

Charles Heidsieck 'Mis en Cave 1993' NV 13 H

Bottoms Up only.

Charles Heidsieck 'Mis en Cave 1994' NV 13 H

Bottoms Up only.

**Cool Ridge Sparkling Chardonnay Pinot
Noir Brut NV (Hungary)** 11 C

Not a sparkling wine to offer anyone you wish to impress or
persuade.

Cordon Negro Freixenet Brut 1993 (Spain) | 16 | D

Great price for such boldness of style and subtle flavour. Has finesse and class.

Cordon Negro Freixenet Medium Dry (Spain) | 14.5 | D

Deutz Marlborough Cuvee (New Zealand) | 15 | E

Delicious – no other word for it.

Drappier Carte d'Or Brut | 12 | G

Jean de Praisac Brut | 13 | F

Le Mesnil Grand Cru, Blanc de Blancs 1990 | 15 | G

Lindauer Brut (New Zealand) | 13.5 | D

Lindauer Brut Rose (New Zealand) | 14 | D

Lindauer Special Reserve NV (New Zealand) | 14 | E

An echo of peach but it's essentially dry and very stylish.

Mercier Vintage Champagne 1990 | 15 | H

A gorgeous bottle of subtle yet rich bubbly. A real treat for rich sybarites.

Moet's Green Point Brut 1995 (USA) | 15 | F

Rather haughty in its richness and grand Champagne-style maturity. Not at Thresher Wine Shops.

Moet's Green Point Rose 1993 (USA) `12` `F`

Not at Thresher Wine Shops.

Moet's Shadow Creek Blanc de Noirs NV `14` `E`

Under a tenner, it's better than Moet & Chandon's French efforts.

Mumm Cuvee Napa Brut (California) `15` `E`

Mumm Cuvee Napa Rose (California) `14` `E`

Out of the Blue Lightly Sparkling (Italy) (4%) `13` `B`

A screw cap bubbly! Super sipping for the simperingly palated.

Perrier-Jouet Brut Vintage 1992 `12` `H`

Too much! Too much! Get thee to a health farm, price tag!

'PG' Pinot Grigio Frizzante `10` `C`

Somewhat toothless.

Pol Roger Champagne White Foil `11` `H`

Ruinart Champagne 1990 `13.5` `H`

Touch of class. But twenty-six quid's a lot of money. Not at Thresher Wine Shops.

Seaview Pinot Noir/Chardonnay 1994 (Australia) `16` `E`

One of Australia's strongest and tastiest challenges to Rheims' hegemony.

Seppelt Great Western Brut (Australia)   13.5   D

Still a bargain. Elegant and dry.

Yalumba Pinot Noir Chardonnay Brut   16   E

Quite delicious. Perhaps a touch soft to seduce or convince the classicist but its quality and style, to me at least, sing out.

UNWINS

EVERY WINE A DUFF ONE! AND WAS THAT A
ROLFE IN SHEEP'S CLOTHING? (OR WAS THE
SUIT SILK?)

It's two years since Unwins bought Davisons' chain of wine shops and the effects of going out and spending a lot on a new toy has at last animated and excited this long-established and once sleepy retailer (established four years before the British Museum). Cynics will say – of course – that because Unwins paid me good money to write the introduction to its summer wine list this year that I'm nothing more than a stooge who won't say anything critical in the hope of being asked back again next year but the fact is Unwins *has* changed. The shops are gaudy, well positioned for the most part, and the range of wines is improving in breadth and depth. Revolution is not in the air but certainly reform is and, as history teaches us, it is the latter style of instrument which is often the surer engine of change. Revolutions tend to throw out the baby with the bath water.

Mr Gerald Duff, Unwins purchasing and marketing director, and his colleague, Mr Bill Rolfe, sales and marketing director, have kept their baby: a chain of southern based wine shops, fattened up via the Davisons acquisition, and if the bath water has not entirely been thrown out, it is surely trickling steadily away. That, dear bargain seeker, is about the strength of it. Gossip or ground breaking developments from these discreet and down-to-earth gentlemen are not yet forthcoming. But, they assure me, lots of exciting new wines are on the way.

If nothing else, Mr Rolfe personally proved to me and to himself the efficacy of using white wine to remove the stain caused by red. When I blundered into Unwins big branch in Camden Town during the summer to attend a wine tasting, there were Messrs Duff and Rolfe, handsomely suited, ready and waiting for me. My bike bag, however, is a notorious non-respecter of persons and it flew from my hands and neatly uprooting three bottles of red as emphatically as South Africa's bowlers did English stumps cascaded a measure of the red stuff over the latter's rather natty lower habiliments. Naturally, I was shocked. But Mr Rolfe, declaring himself much amused, calmly permitted white wine to be poured over himself and, an hour later, not a stain was to be seen.

'Nice to have a bit of excitement at one of our tastings,' he said. But I do wonder what he said to Mr Duff about cack-handed wine writers once I had clambered back on my bike and pedalled off down the street.

Unwins Wine Group Limited
Birchwood House
Victoria Road
Dartford
Kent DA1 5AJ
Tel: 01322 272711
Fax: 01322 294469

ARGENTINIAN WINE

RED

Magdalena River Malbec/Cabernet Sauvignon, Mendoza 1997

14 C

Very juicy and ripe but again with that curious finish of great dryness. Good with food.

Magdalena River Sangiovese/Bonarda, Mendoza 1997

14.5 C

Deliciously invigorating wine of substance, richness and texture. The wine finishes positively and well and very dryly.

Santa Julia Malbec Oak Reserve, Mendoza 1995

14 D

Juicy, yes, but it's got wood and tannin propping it well and decisively.

ARGENTINIAN WINE

WHITE

Magdalena River Chardonnay, Mendoza 1997

15.5 C

Big and meaty with a hedgerow fruitiness underlined by a suggestion of twig. Great food wine.

AUSTRALIAN WINE · RED

Bethany Pressings Grenache, Barossa Valley 1995
`14.5` `D`

Very ripe and vanillary, jammy and lively. Great glugging to turn a blue mood to a rich red.

Brown Brothers Tarrango 1997
`15` `D`

Beaujolais in all but name. Or rather Beaujolais as it might be – given the fruit.

Caversham Cabernet/Shiraz 1995
`13.5` `E`

David Wynn Cabernet Sauvignon, S. Australia 1997
`14` `D`

Loads of flavour and baked fruit – as if it was left bruised on the ground before pressing. The result is exuberance and great richness.

Grant Burge Old Vine Barossa Shiraz 1996
`16` `E`

Medicinal, minty, polished, plummy, thickly textured, savoury, dry, gorgeous.

Maglieri Shiraz, McLaren Vale 1996
`14` `E`

Has some suggestion of the soppiness of the Aussie shiraz in its softly softly mode but this example is saved on the brink of banality by its tannin.

Mount Langi Ghiran Billi Billi Creek Shiraz/Cabernet Sauvignon 1996
`12` `E`

Silli Silli Creek more like.

Penfolds Rawson's Retreat Bin 35
Cabernet/Shiraz/Ruby Cabernet 1996 `15.5` `D`

Rich, layered, clinging, ripe – a great steak and kidney pudding wine.

Stockman's Bridge Shiraz/Cabernet
Sauvignon `12.5` `C`

AUSTRALIAN WINE WHITE

Brown Bothers Chenin Blanc 1997 `15` `C`

An exotic chenin with a hint of sweet fruit but with oriental food it's a terrific proposition. Try it with duck and plum sauce.

CV Unwooded Chardonnay, Western
Australia 1997 `16.5` `E`

This is the year, '97, to wallow in the richness of the Aussie chardonnay, especially when no wood is aboard and the provenance is Western Australia. A gloriously uncluttered, elegant wine of potency, finesse and heavenly texture.

David Wynn Chardonnay, S. Australia 1997 `16` `D`

Expensive treat here. A rich, almost oily, chardonnay with a bare hint of exoticism on its finish but mostly just good, home-baked fruit.

Grant Burge Old Vine Semillon, Barossa
Valley 1997 `14` `E`

Good lingering creaminess with a hint of nut. Touch expensive.

Ironstone Semillon/Chardonnay 1997 15 D

One of Western Australia's most poignant expressions of semillon. Lovely fish wine.

Lindemans Botrytis Riesling 1996 (half bottle) 16.5 D

Gorgeous richness of honeydew melon saturated with waxy honey and pineapple. A hugely sweet, tart white wine of style and great longevity. It will develop in bottle for twenty years.

Penfolds Rawsons Retreat Bin 21 Semillon/Chardonnay/Colombard 1997 15 C

The gorgeously rich '97 vintage strikes the palate with polish, purpose and plumpness.

Saltram Mamre Brook Chardonnay 1995 14.5 D

Stockman's Bridge Semillon/Chardonnay NV 13.5 C

Bit muted on the finish.

Tyrrell's Vat 47 Pinot Chardonnay 1995 13 F

BULGARIAN WINE RED

Cabernet Sauvignon/Merlot Reserve, Suhindol 1993 C

Dry and a touch reluctant on the finish.

Country Wine Merlot/Pinot Noir NV, Sliven

Cheap and cheerful. Wonderfully dry and home-spun but great with bangers.

Domaine Boyar Merlot, Iambol 1997

All fruit, zippy, fun, laid-back.

BULGARIAN WINE WHITE

Barrel Fermented Chardonnay 1996

The wood strains for effect on the finish. And the strain shows.

Country Wine Muskat & Ugni Blanc, Shumen NV

A deliciously delicate, floral-scented aperitif wine.

Premium Oak Barrel Fermented Chardonnay, Shumen 1997

Don't find the wood puts up a hugely convincing case for itself.

CHILEAN WINE RED

Carmen Cabernet Sauvignon 1996

Extruded length to the fruit – it seems to stretch itself, languid and delicious, from tongue tip to adenoid. A very classy claret-like wine but a very warm, generous one.

Domaine Oriental Clos Centenaire Merlot, Maule Valley 1997

Finishes a touch dry and the fruit seems casual here, but the initial attack is positive and richly flavoured.

Errazuriz Syrah Reserve, Aconcagua 1997

Smoke and baked ham assail the nostrils and rich damson the tongue. It's finest moment is in its death throes when the tannins clock in and the wine expires gorgeously in the throat.

Gracia Merlot Reserve, Aconcagua 1997

Huge depth of flavour here, leather/blackcurrant/plum, and great developed tannins. Brilliant tone, polish, character and style.

La Palma Merlot 1997 16 C

Elegant but very full and deep. Finishes dry but it starts with vigour and style.

Morande Merlot/Syrah, Rapel 1997 13 D

CHILEAN WINE WHITE

Domaine Oriental Clos Centenaire Chardonnay, Maule Valley 1997

Not as elegant as other Chilean chardonnays but it does have a sticky richness of texture which might adhere nicely to food.

Domaine Oriental Sauvignon Blanc, Maule Valley 1997

What finesse and class here: delicious delicacy and litheness. Not a big, rich, grassy sauvignon but a beautifully textured one of real style.

Errazuriz Wild Ferment Chardonnay, Casablanca 1997

16.5 E

Wonderful that the wine should wish to keep its cork as its only synthetic touch, thus preserving from natural cork taint the delicate, natural fruitiness of what is a lovely, understated wine. Many Chilean chardonnays at half the price of this one are fruitier but this is not about sheer fruit. This wine is about texture, very subtle complexity and flavours you have to search for.

Gracia Chardonnay Reserve, Cachapoal 1997

15.5 E

Impressively woody, vanillary chardonnay with layers of interwoven flavour and textured immediacy. Very classy feel to this wine.

ENGLISH WINE
WHITE

Lamberhurst Sovereign Medium Dry

Three Choirs Estate Premium 1993

FRENCH WINE   RED

Ash Ridge Cabernet Sauvignon/Merlot d'Oc 1996   15   C

Lovely polished texture.

Ash Ridge Cabernet Sauvignon/Syrah d'Oc 1996   15   C

Smoky richness and depth. Delicious.

Ash Ridge Merlot d'Oc 1997   14   C

Cigar smoke edge to the finish which is soft and lush.

Bergerac Comtesse Catherine 1996   13.5   C

Bourgueil Les Barroirs, Couly-Dutheil 1995   13.5   D

Burgundy Pinot Noir Albert Bichot 1995   10   D

Cabardes Chateau Ventenac, Alain Maurel 1996   14.5   C

Real dry, violet-edged fruit of character and warmth. Terrific food wine.

Cabrieres, Coteaux du Languedoc 1996   13   C

Touch ho-hum on the finish.

Chateau Astruc Minervois 1997   14   C

It's the texture which wins it. It's superbly polished and plump. A real mouthful of fruit.

Chateau Courteau Mauregard, Bordeaux 1996　　14　C

Chateau du Perier Medoc Cru Bourgeois 1996　　12　E

Very dry and austere, but not in a claret-like way, rather a raw, underdeveloped way. A very closed wine. Maybe a few years in bottle will open it up.

Chateau du Pin St Martial Borie-Manoux, Bordeaux 1995　　12　C

Chinon Les Gravieres, Couly-Dutheil 1996　　14　D

Claret Special Reserve Yvon Mau 1996　　13　C

Faugeres Domaine d'Azil 1997　　16　C

Real character, warmth, herbiness, dryness and savoury depth here. Great value tannins, worth the price of admission alone.

Fitou Chateau de Segure 1995　　13.5　C

La Cigaliere Cotes du Rhone 1997　　13　C

Bit costive.

Les Beaux Sites Domaine de Bernou 1996　　15.5　D

Real cab franc flavour and varietal impact.

Les Beaux Sites Domaine de Castan 1996　　16　C

Lovely soft texture and tannins, great flavour and approachability.

Les Beaux Sites Domaine de Robert 1995　　16.5　C

Knocks Australia into a cocked hat for under a fiver. A rich wine of such depth, flavour, style and tannic perfection, it should make Australia tremble.

Lirac Domaine Duseigneur 1996 `13` `D`

Oddly juicy for a Lirac.

Madiran Chateau de Crouseilles 1990 `15.5` `E`

A wine of great depth and woody richness but it's not the richness of precision and neatly tailored fruit but of raunchy tannicity and a great embrace of energy. A delicious, very dry wine of immense food matching qualities.

Morgon 'Cave Bocabarteille' 1997 `10` `D`

Rivesaltes Vintage Les Producteurs Reunis 1996 `15` `C`

An interesting sweet red wine to drink with ripe cheeses, fruit, summer pudding, or watching the Lottery Draw on TV. Wrong numbers again? This ripe, raisiny brew might not be for you, either.

FRENCH WINE WHITE

Anjou Blanc Jean Sablenay 1997 `13.5` `B`

A touch tarty but not unattractive.

Ash Ridge Grenache Viognier d'Oc 1997 `15.5` `C`

Gorgeous hint of spice and a gentle floreate fruitiness which is never overblown or blowsy. Delicious.

Bergerac Comtesse Catherine 1997　13　B

Very grassy.

Bordeaux Sauvignon Yvon Mau 1996　13.5　C

Burgundy Chardonnay Albert Bichot 1996　11　D

Chateau Ducla Entre Deux Mers 1996　14　C

Chateau Mire l'Etang, Coteaux du Languedoc La Clape 1997 (oaked)　12　C

Somewhat flat and cloddish on the finish.

Corbieres Les Producteurs du Mont Tauch　12　C

Gewurztraminer Reserve Personelle, Kuentz-Bas 1993　15.5　E

Delicious full-throated, toffee-attack of rose-petal fruit, soft and lush, but with an elegance of finish which gives it class (and its rating at a tenner a bottle).

Les Trois Herault Les Chais Beaucarois NV　13　B

Very fruity – almost demi-sec. Not sure it's serious enough to rate higher.

Muscadet sur Lie Pierre Brevin 1997　13.5　C

A richer, more textured Muscadet than most.

Rose d'Anjou, Celliers du Prieure 1997　12　B

Bit cosmetic and jammy for me.

Sancerre Jean Sablenay 1997　12　E

The cheek of Sancerre asking this price. Chile does it better, much better, for half the price.

GREEK WINE · WHITE

Retsina of Attica 'Kourtaki' | 13 | B

Samos Vin Doux Naturel, Kourtakis NV | 13.5 | C

HUNGARIAN WINE · RED

Blue Remembered Hills Blauer Zweigelt 1997 | 12 | C

Not quite as memorable as its makers might hope for. But not entirely best forgotten.

Volcanic Hills Kekfrancos 1997 | 13 | C

HUNGARIAN WINE · WHITE

Chapel Hill Irsai Oliver, Balatonboglar 1997 | 13.5 | B

Makes a delicate little companion for baked cod.

Chapel Hill Oaked Chardonnay, Balatonboglar 1997 | 13 | C

Touch dullish on the finish. Seems unsure of where to go.

ITALIAN WINE — RED

Montepulciano d'Abruzzo Miglianico 1996 `13` `C`

Sangiovese di Puglia, Vigneti di Sole 1997 `13` `C`

ITALIAN WINE — WHITE

Alasia Chardonnay del Piemonte 1997 `13` `C`

Cerveteri Bianco 1996 `12` `C`

Est! Est!! Est!!! di Monte Fiascone 1996 `12` `C`

Frascati Superiore Selezione, Tullio San
Marco 1996 `13.5` `D`

Frascati Superiore, Tullio San Marco 1996 `11` `C`

Gavi Antario 1996 `13` `D`

NEW ZEALAND WINE — RED

Ata Rangi Celebre 1995 `13` `F`

Delegat's Hawkes Bay Cabernet
Sauvignon/Merlot 1996 `13` `D`

Bit of a juicy vintage.

Sacred Hill Basket Press Merlot/Cabernet, Hawkes Bay 1995   `13.5` `E`

Soft and giggly.

NEW ZEALAND WINE   WHITE

Marlborough Gold Sauvignon Blanc 1997   `15` `C`

Hints of rich grass with a full-throated texture of taste-bud-coating tenacity.

Oyster Bay Sauvignon Blanc, Marlborough 1997   `16` `D`

Classic sauvignon dryness and sense of humour. Finishes with purpose and aplomb.

Sacred Hill Barrique Fermented Chardonnay 1996   `15.5` `E`

Woody, chewy, busy, bright, soft yet with a hint of crispness, this is a very giving, rich wine of weight and wit.

Seifried Estate Sauvignon Blanc, Nelson 1997   `13.5` `D`

Finishes a touch muddily.

PORTUGUESE WINE   RED

Alta Mesa Estremadura 1995   `15.5` `B`

Baga Bella Fonte 1997 `12.5` `C`

Finishes a bit spinelessly – considering the feel of the fruit as it first impacts.

Garrafeira Reserva Particular, A Bernardino 1987 `13` `D`

Portada 1996 `13` `C`

Very juicy.

Quinta da Foz de Arouce 1995 `16` `F`

One of the richest, fruitiest, best balanced, most firmly tannically exciting Portuguese reds around.

Quinta das Setencostas, Alenquer Region 1997 `14` `C`

Very juicy and ripe. The tannins are a well-kept secret until well after the fruit has gone, jammily, down the throat.

PORTUGUESE WINE WHITE

Bical Bella Fonte 1997 `15` `C`

Unusual grape variety, the bical, and it tastes a bit Alsatian in its richness and textural ripeness, but with fewer floral overtones. An interesting wine of individuality and style. A good food wine.

Chardonnay Casa Lantos Lima 1996 `11` `D`

SOUTH AFRICAN WINE   RED

Beyerskloof Pinotage, Stellenbosch 1997 · 14 · D

Juicy, rubbery, joyous.

Clos Malverne Cabernet/Shiraz, Stellenbosch 1997 · 10 · D

I simply don't find the medicinal overtones attractive.

Glen Carlou Merlot 1996 · 13.5 · E

Lot of loot for a wine of the fiver class (at the most).

Hidden River Pinotage NV · 14 · C

Hidden River Ruby Cabernet NV · 13.5 · C

SOUTH AFRICAN WINE   WHITE

Boschendal Sauvignon Blanc, Paarl 1996 · 13 · D

Not as brilliant as it has been.

Hidden River Chardonnay NV · 11 · C

Hidden River Chenin Blanc NV · 11 · C

Hidden River Sauvignon Blanc NV · 12 · C

Jordan Chardonnay, Stellenbosch 1997 · 13.5 · E

Too expensive for the lack of direction on the finish.

SPANISH WINE   RED

Don Fabian Tempranillo Navarra 1995   `14` `C`

Faustino Rivero Ulecia Rioja 1992   `14` `D`

Stowells of Chelsea Tempranillo (3-litre box) `14` `B`

Price bracket has been adjusted to reflect the bottle equivalent.

Val de Borja Garnacha 1997   `14.5` `C`

Light, at first impact, then the fruit gathers pace and pressure and it finishes with tannic aplomb and a hint of spiced plum.

SPANISH WINE   WHITE

El Coto Rioja 1995   `13.5` `D`

USA WINE   RED

De Loach Zinfandel Platinum 1996   `11` `E`

Not up to a lot for eight quid. Fruit juicy and simple minded.

Easton Zinfandel, Shenandoah Valley 1995 `11` `E`

Juice, lots of juice.

Ironstone Vineyards Cabernet Franc 1995 `13.5` `D`

Touch expensive for the juiciness.

M G Vallejo Pinot Noir 1995 `12.5` `D`

USA WINE WHITE

Blossom Hill NV, California `10` `C`

Echo Ridge Fume Blanc 1996 `15.5` `C`

My God! Doesn't it put many Pouillys to shame! Rich yet elegant, interesting smoky edge.

Fetzer Viognier 1997 `15.5` `E`

Shows how firmly fruity viognier can become, warmly encouraged to this level of expression by the Californian sun.

Gallo French Colombard `9` `C`

FORTIFIED WINE

Calem 10 Year Old Port `11` `G`

Rather sweet and expensively uncomplex.

Calem LBV Port 1993 `11` `E`

Rather undistinguished for the money.

Dom Ramos Manzanilla `14.5` `C`

Dos Cortados Dry Old Oloroso Sherry `14` `E`

Intensely dry and curious. Like a joke told in an English gentlemens' club. Chilled with nuts and olives is its milieu.

Matusalem Sweet Old Oloroso Sherry `14.5` `E`

Linctusy thick and lush. When to drink it? On your death bed – the grim reaper can oil his scythe with it.

SPARKLING WINE/CHAMPAGNE

Angas Rose Brut (Australia) `15.5` `D`

Carrington Extra Brut (Australia) `13.5` `D`

Cava Brut Methode Traditionelle `14` `D`

Chardonnay Blanc de Blancs 'Le Baron' Brut `13.5` `D`

Cremant de Bourgogne Chardonnay Brut `13` `E`

Duchatel Blanc de Blancs Champagne `11` `G`

Duchatel Brut Champagne NV `12` `F`

Graham Beck Brut, Madeba Valley (South Africa) `13` `E`

Graham Beck Chardonnay/Pinot Noir (South Africa) `13` `D`

Lindauer Brut (New Zealand) `13.5` `D`

Nicolas Feuillate Brut Premier Cru NV `14` `G`

Seaview Brut Rose `15` `D`

Stockman's Bridge Brut (Australia) `12` `D`

Bit adolescent.

Yalumba Pinot Noir/Chardonnay (Australia) `16` `E`

One of the Antipodes' finest.

VICTORIA WINE

EXODUS! BUT CAN THE NEW FACES TURN VW INTO A PORSCHE?

It was widely reported last year in the financial press that Allied Domecq, which owns Victoria Wine, was rumoured to be looking for a buyer for the chain. This followed the announcement that VW's trading profits had fallen by £3m over the preceding trading period. Allied Domecq did not comment officially on the market rumours (why would it?), so people like me can only speculate.

The chain itself had some of its wine buying department poached by other retailers, but got aggressively into some excellent multiple purchase offers on wine (two bottles for a fiver, that sort of thing), brought in some new blood, and thanks to the energy of its wine PR manager, Nicola Harvey, has managed to give a fair account of itself. I don't have the latest VW financial figures to hand to confirm whether profits are more buoyant, but growth in sales, on the basis of statistics supplied to me by the chain, suggests that the bullish attitude here is not entirely based on hope over expectation. However, whenever I ask a supermarket head wine buyer how sales are going compared to wine shops I receive a picture which, if it is to be believed, leads to a scenario suggesting that by early next century there won't be any off-licence shops in existence (apart from licensed corner-shop grocers) only specialists like VW's Wine Cellars, Wine Rack, Oddbins and Bottoms Up plus a few regional others.

As an organisation, VW doesn't seem to be letting any grass

grow under its feet. Its various expansion ideas, all put in place over the past year, sound ambitious yet realistic. It has, for example, launched a home shopping scheme. Victoria Wine Cellars Direct, as it is called, was tested as an idea in the West Midlands last year.

VW also opened the Martha's Vineyard drinks superstore – 5,000 sq ft of shelves at New Barnet in Hertfordshire. It is a bid to tackle the dominance by the supermarkets of the UK's £7 billion take-home drinks market (according to some estimates supermarkets now control 60% but supermarket own figures put it at over 70%). The superstore has 650 wines and there is a 10% discount on large purchases. VW says it is targeting people who do not currently use VW stores but may buy their drinks at supermarkets. Three more stores are planned for 1998. (Some months later, Thresher closed its warehouse concept, Booze Barn, while Oddbins launched its first warehouse store.) The company has said that sales at its Martha's Vineyard are 'bang on target' and confirmed that more stores would open.

Last year, Victoria Wine became the first branded off-licence to open a forecourt outlet. The lucky site was a Total petrol station in Addlestone in Surrey. Alcohol Concern was appalled, saying that it would conflict with anti-drink driving messages but even as this book went to press there are several hundred petrol forecourts holding liquor licences.

VW also opened its 100th Victoria Wine Cellars outlet in Winchester. Seems to have taken them quite a long time to get to Winchester – given that the stores are aimed at the ABC1 demographic profile. As of November 1997, around half of the Cellars stores were in the south of England. But expansion to other parts of the UK is planned. A further fifty or so VW Cellars stores are supposed to be opening in the next two years. Present total is around 120 Cellars.

Earlier this year, January 1998, in a link-up with NSPCC, VW launched a wine called The Italian Job (red and white retailing at £3.99). For every case sold £1 goes to the charity which hopes to raise £30,000 over the next three years. A fairly modest sum based on VW's expecting to sell 10,000 cases a year. The chain also gained some mild notoriety for its Football Red and Football White (for reasons which escaped me). It also became the sole distributor for the officially approved France '98 Champagne, which I for one found underfruited and overpriced.

By now, the retailer had two petrol station outlets trading and it was reported that Victoria Wine was looking to move into forecourt retailing in a big way and the usual rumours circulated; VW being said to be in discussions with both petrol station and convenience store operators about possible partnerships. By the summer of 1998, the retailer reported wine sales up 12% and reported 'encouraging' results with its Martha's Vineyard and petrol forecourt activities. Profits for that half of the financial year, increased by £1m.

Of the experience of actually buying wine at VW outlets, I can only report that this year has been a good one for my postman Gerry. As the chap who has to shove readers' letters through my door, he often has to stand on the front step for so long poking the envelopes through the flap (when I am not in to open the door to him) that he has taken to bringing a collapsible bed with him rather than stand out there all day and all night. If during the week following the appearance of a VW bargain wine in my Saturday *Guardian* column I receive no letters, I take that to mean happy readers. If, however, readers are faced with mute incomprehension by shop staff when asking for a well recommended wine, as has happened in the past, the letters flood in. VW has not occasioned a single letter all year (at time of writing).

Long may this continue. I sometimes feel like an agony aunt when I read some readers' letters.

Victoria Wine Co
Dukes Court
Duke Street
Woking
Surrey GU21 5XL
Tel: 01483 715066
Fax: 01483 755234

**SEE STOP PRESS SECTION AT END OF BOOK FOR
LAST-MINUTE ADDITIONS OR UPDATES TO THIS
RETAILER'S RANGE.**

ARGENTINIAN WINE RED

Balbi Vineyards Malbec 1997 14 | C

Juicy and rich, as all Balbi's wines seem to be. It bounces around the taste buds like a big bonny bowl of fruit (dryish).

Bright Brother Argentine Tempranillo 1997 15 | C

Rather haughty in its own dry way. It's a delicious sipping wine, perhaps too dry for some, but the rich plum fruit is great with food. Wine Cellar stores only.

Las Lilas Malbec Syrah 1997 14.5 | C

A heady broth of boot polish, ripe plums, cherries and some kind of nut. Very deep, very savoury.

Marge 'n' Tina Malbec/Tempranillo 1997 13.5 | C

Should be £3.49 not £4.49. Pity, this discrepancy. Its cheek both as a label and as a richly fruity wine is engaging.

Martin's Andino Malbec Bonarda 1997 14 | C

How to make dry, sophisticated super plonk. Grow the fruit in Argentina! And get spiciness and sauciness yet seriousness.

Valentin Bianchi Cabernet Sauvignon 1995 16 | E

Very aromatic, juicy yet richly textured and dry to finish, this is a concentrated classic cabernet of utterly seductive drinkability. Not at all stores.

ARGENTINIAN WINE WHITE

Correas Torrontes Chardonnay 1997

Superb clash of fruit styles in the mouth, cleanness and appleyness on one side and hints of raspberry and peach on the other, but they combine on the finish as vigorous and fresh.

Santa Julia Chardonnay 1998

Touch uncertain and even a bit ragged on the finish. Quibbles? Maybe, but at this close to a fiver more polish is required to rate higher. Not at all stores.

Valentin Bianchi Chardonnay 1996

Elegant, ripe, rich, positive yet rather exciting and warm on the finish, where it becomes passionate and very fruity. But it's a lovely wine. Only at Wine Cellar stores.

AUSTRALIAN WINE RED

Brown Brothers Merlot, King Valley 1995

Curious merlot (especially at this price). It's merlot as old-fashioned premier cru Beaujolais. Exceedingly quaffable.

Brown Brothers Tarrango 1997

Sweet and swinging. A night club wine, where hot lights, cigarette smoke, and Salsa music (and dips) combine to encourage the belief that an adult drink is in the glass.

Hardys Bankside Shiraz 1996

Has some ruggedness to its essentially easy-going character.

Hardys Nottage Hill Cabernet Sauvignon/ Shiraz 1996

Elegant, rich, aromatic, balanced, most compellingly well priced, and more stylish than other vintages of the same brand.

Hardys Stamp Series Shiraz Cabernet Sauvignon 1997

Touch soupy and puppyish but hugely drinkable.

Leasingham Grenache 1996

Ripeness but there are some rare tannins here, and nuttiness. Good food wine. Wine Cellars and Martha's Vineyard only.

Penfolds Kalimna Shiraz Bin 28 1994

Penfolds Old Vine Barossa Valley Shiraz/Grenache/Mourvedre 1994

The Aussie answer to Chateauneuf-du-Pape? If so, there's something for the Frogs to chew on here: dryness (with a subtle herbiness), richness (with great depth of flavour), balance, style and loads of well toned fruit. Goes with food and mood. A rousing bottle of ten quid well spent.

Rosemount Cabernet Sauvignon, Hunter Valley 1996

Big, juicy, rich.

Salisbury Estate Grenache 1996

Saltram Shiraz 1996

Soup, pure invalid's soup.

Shirazamatazz 1996   15   D

At last, a jazzily labelled red which lives up to its name. A rich, warm, 15-point red of richness, beautifully soft yet insistent tannins and deep, sunny fruit. A warming wine indeed.

Thomas Mitchell Shiraz 1996   14   D

Juicy, savoury, touch soupy. But deeply quaffable.

Wynn's Coonawarra Shiraz 1996   D

Cool minty undertones to some impressively meaty fruit which carries a hint of proper tannin. Terrific Aussie shiraz at a decent price.

AUSTRALIAN WINE   WHITE

Brokenback Ridge Chardonnay 1998

Almost in the class of a Chilean chardonnay, under four quid! It has flavour, texture and lingering warmth and freshness. Not at all stores.

Brown Brothers Chenin Blanc 1997   15   C

An exotic chenin with a hint of sweet fruit but with oriental food it's a terrific proposition. Try it with duck and plum sauce.

Hardys Nottage Hill Chardonnay 1997 ⟮16.5⟯ ⟮C⟯

Fantastic oily/buttery texture, ripe fruit, just terrific.

Jacobs Creek Semillon Chardonnay 1997 ⟮14⟯ ⟮C⟯

Old Aussie warhorse, still soldiering on.

Koala Falls Chardonnay/Semillon 1997 ⟮13.5⟯ ⟮C⟯

Lindemans Bin 70 Semillon/Verdelho/ Sauvignon Blanc/Chardonnay 1997 ⟮15⟯ ⟮C⟯

Brilliant soft spiciness for oriental food.

Lindemans Botrytis Riesling 1996 (half bottle) ⟮16.5⟯ ⟮D⟯

Gorgeous richness of honeydew melon saturated with waxy honey and pineapple. A hugely sweet, tart white wine of style and great longevity. It will develop in bottle for twenty years.

Lindemans Padthaway Chardonnay 1996 ⟮15.5⟯ ⟮E⟯

Mitchelton Chardonnay 1996 ⟮15⟯ ⟮E⟯

Depth of flavour, warmth, steady output of rolling fruit – this is an engaging wine of substance and creamy deliciousness.

Penfolds Rawsons Retreat Bin 21 Semillon/Chardonnay/Colombard 1997 ⟮15⟯ ⟮C⟯

The gorgeously rich '97 vintage strikes the palate with polish, purpose and plumpness.

Thomas Mitchell Marsanne 1996 ⟮14⟯ ⟮D⟯

A food wine preeminently: rich, savoury, well-textured.

Wolf Blass Riesling 1997

Try it with tandoori prawns. You may swoon with pleasure.

BULGARIAN WINE RED

Bulgarian Cabernet Sauvignon, Sliven 1993

Good bangers and mash plonk. Firm, rich, bright, with-it.

Bulgarian Country Wine Cabernet Sauvignon/Merlot Pavlikeni NV

Fruity fun for curry eaters.

Bulgarian Vintners' Cabernet Sauvignon Rubin, Plovdiv 1996

Bulgarian Vintners Reserve Cabernet Sauvignon 1991

Ripe and polished with a hint of dirty boot. So: swig it or glug it with food. Pasta with a rich sauce, say.

Bulgarian Vintners Sliven & Pinot Noir NV

Somewhat peppery and jammy but, chilled, you have good value glugging here.

Liubimetz Merlot 1996

Magnificent dry, herby beast of depth, richness and balance (tannins and fruit). It has class, quaffability, food compatibility, yet true complex structure. Terrific.

Lovico Suhindol Merlot/Gamza Country Wine NV

14 B

Stowells Bulgarian Red (3-litre box)

11 B

Price band has been adjusted to show bottle equivalent.

Suhindol Special Reserve Cabernet Sauvignon 1992

15 C

BULGARIAN WINE WHITE

Chardonnay/Aligote, Pavlikeni NV

15.5 B

Brilliant value for Christmas at two for a fiver. A gentle, fresh, modern wine of considerable charm, good manner, and gentle fruit. Delicious simplicity.

CHILEAN WINE RED

Altura Cabernet Sauvignon 1997

15 C

Dry, biscuity texture with a rich fruit coating. Deeply quaffable and with some seriousness on the finish.

Caliterra Reserva Cabernet Sauvignon 1995

17 D

Utterly captivating fruit here. It grabs hold of the molars with cassis-edged yet dry tenacity and provokes immediate cranial excitement. Great stuff.

Canepa Cabernet Sauvignon 1998

Rather a juicy cabernet for a fiver. Only at Wine Cellar stores.

Concha y Toro Casillero del Diablo
Cabernet Sauvignon 1996

Deeper, darker, more exotic than previous vintages, this cabernet is very savoury and rich, subdued tannically, and with a softness yet solidity of great class.

Concha y Toro Merlot/Malbec 1998

Young yet but the tannins and rich leathery, spicy fruit are in tremendous harmony. Will improve vividly over the next twelve to eighteen months, but no longer. Not at all stores.

Cono Sur Merlot 1997

With its terrific plastic cork this wine is in perfect taint-free condition to soothe the taste buds with its lovely texture, hint of leather, rich ripe fruit and accomplished finish.

Cono Sur Pinot Noir 1996

Santa Rita Petite Syrah Merlot 1997 | 16 | D |

Such thickness of jammy yet dry, classy fruit. The tannins are beautifully clotted, the fruit is as textured as double whipped cream. Not at all stores.

Santa Rita Reserva Merlot 1996 | 16 | D |

Compelling richness and texture, classy fruit, longevity of finish and delicious, serious balance of elements. Not at all stores.

CHILEAN WINE   WHITE

Canepa Oak Aged Semillon 1996   15.5   C

Coba Falls Chilean Dry White NV   15   B

**Concha y Toro Casillero del Diablo
Chardonnay 1996**   16   C

Stunning lushness and poise. This is, perhaps, the double-whammy which characterises Chilean style with chardonnay: impact yet deftness.

Cono Sur Gewurztraminer 1997   15   C

Dry, hint of spice, fresh, gushing yet restrained. Delicious.

Errazuriz Sauvignon Blanc 1996   15.5   C

La Palma Chardonnay 1997   16   C

Wonderful value: opulent, textured, ripe, discreet yet exuberant, and lushly flavoured yet chic and sophisticated as it settles in the back of the throat. Not at all stores.

Los Caneses Sauvignon Blanc 1998   16   C

Rather a delicate flower and extremely lightly coloured. Will it attract the right insects? Well, it got to this bumble bee in the end by the persistence of its elegance and subtle charm.

**Stowells of Chelsea Chilean Sauvignon
Blanc (3-litre box)**   15.5   B

Price band has been adjusted to show bottle equivalent.

Vina Casablanca Sauvignon Blanc 1997 `16.5` `D`

What wonderful oily texture, richness yet elegance of finish, what terrific underlying nuttiness! A terrific wine.

ENGLISH WINE WHITE

Summerhill Dry White `11` `C`

FRENCH WINE RED

Beaujolais Philippe de Corcelettes 1997 `11` `C`

Beaune-Toussaints Domaine Rene Monnier 1996 `10` `G`

Jejune juice. Only at Wine Cellar and Martha's Vineyard stores.

Big Frank's Red, Minervois 1996 `13.5` `C`

Calvet Reserve 1995 `14.5` `D`

Has some old-fashioned claret virtues plus a hint of new-fangled fruity modernity. Most accommodating wine.

Charles d'Hauteville Oak Aged Claret NV `12.5` `C`

Charles de France Bourgogne Pinot Noir 1996 `11` `D`

Pretentious in name, label, bottle . . . but no pretensions to the fruit.

Chateau Beauvoisin, Costieres de Nimes 1995　16　C

Real swashbuckling richness, flavour, individuality and style here. Great balance of elements with fruit emerging the flavoursome winner over tannins and acidity. Wine Cellars and Martha's Vineyard only.

Chateau de Clostre, Bordeaux Superieur 1995　13　D

Lot of money. Needs time, this wine. But even then it ought to be cheaper.

Chateau de l'Abbaye de Saint Ferme Bordeaux Superieur 1996　15　D

Chateau de Vaudieu, Chateauneuf-du-Pape 1995　16　F

Impressive hauteur here: rich, deep, superbly polished, complex, delicate yet potent.

Chateau Haut Marbuzet, St Estephe 1995　15　H

Expensive treat for Christmas? Just about. Worth the money for the tannins. They are in a class which tells you all about St Estephe. Only at Wine Cellar and Martha's Vineyard stores.

Chateau La Jalgue, Bordeaux 1996　15　C

Claret 1997, Victoria Wine　14　C

Friendlier than normal, this is a fine little glugging claret of immediate charm.

Clos Fourquet Cotes de Castillon 1996　12.5　E

I'd rather drink this wine in five years. It will have acquired sageness by then, and, paradoxically, lost its greenness. Wine Cellars and Martha's Vineyard only.

Cornas Les Nobles Rives, Cotes de Tain 1994

Has something to its cigar-edged depth and massively shouldered tannins. Gorgeous texture. Only at Wine Cellar and Martha's Vineyard stores.

Cote Rotie, Domaine de Bonserine 1996

Far too witless and simple-minded to attempt the Times crossword in even thirty minutes. But that's what a £25 price tag is expected to do. Only at Wine Cellar and Martha's Vineyard stores.

Coteaux du Tricastin 1997

Vegetal plump, has some richness.

Domaine de la Grande Bellane, Cotes du Rhone Villages 1996 (organic)

Juicy and very ripe. Touch of earth on the finish.

Domaine de Lions Merlot VdP d'Oc 1997

Has some gritty charm.

Domaine de Peyrat Cabernet Sauvignon Prestige VdP d'Oc 1996

A brilliant depth of flavour here, dark cherryish and ripe but with handsomely integrated tannins, and the finish has aplomb and vigour. Wine Cellars and Martha's Vineyard only.

Domaine de Valette, Saint Chinian 1994 `14.5` `C`

Earthiness meets ripeness. In the struggle, the best arbiter is the intervention of food. Wine Cellars and Martha's Vineyard only.

Fitou Mme Parmentier 1996 `13.5` `C`

Fleurie Duboeuf 1996 `12` `E`

French Full Red VdP d'Oc NV, Victoria Wine `13` `B`

Gamay de Touraine 1997 `14.5` `B`

Delicious, with a hint of vegetal dryness which gives it character without detracting from its bright, gamay-gluggable freshness.

Gevry Chambertin, Domaine Henri Rebourseau 1996 `10` `G`

Oh, come on! Twenty quid?! It's a joke!!! Only at Wine Cellar and Martha's Vineyard stores.

Grenache VdP des Coteaux de l'Ardeche 1997 `14.5` `B`

Excellent price for such approachable earthiness and cherry/plum ripeness (without soppiness).

Hautes Cotes de Nuit 1995 `12` `D`

Hermitage Les Nobles Rives, Cotes de Tain 1994 `11` `G`

Silly price really. The tannins are there but the fruit's gasping to keep up. Only at Wine Cellar and Martha's Vineyard stores.

Julienas Les Fouillouses 1997 `13` `D`

Like the fruit, don't like the price of it.

L'Excellence de Chateau Capendu, Corbieres 1997 `14.5` `D`

Richness and style, a hint of earth. Selected stores.

La Cuvee Mythique Vin de Pays d'Oc 1995 `13.5` `D`

Not in the class of the '94. It's not a poor wine, simply well in excess, money-wise, of the fruit on offer. Wines Cellars only.

Mas de Lunes Coteaux du Languedoc, Domaines JeanJean 1996 `15.5` `C`

Terrific dryness and characterful fruit here. Not elegant or light but neither is it tender-footed – it has weight with wit.

Merlot VdP d'Oc 1997 `13.5` `B`

Begins well, seems to stumble on the finish.

Merlot/Cabernet Sauvignon VdP d'Oc, Bouey 1997 `15.5` `B`

Gorgeous lightness of touch yet seriousness of purpose. This is a fruity red of richness and savour relieved by a sweet fruit edge mingled with a hint of earth and tannin. Terrific quaffer.

Morgon Domaine de Terraine 1996 `10` `D`

Oak Aged Cotes du Rhone, Gabrielle Meffre 1997 `15.5` `C`

Delicious earthy fruit. Classy, modern/ancient, ripe, dry, warm and welcoming.

Pommard, Domaine du Fief de Montjeu 1996

10 G

Wine at this price must be exciting. This is not even vaguely amusing. Only at Wine Cellar and Martha's Vineyard stores.

Roc Saint Vincent Bordeaux 1997

13 C

Has some claret character . . . some.

Saumur Joseph Verdier 1997

14.5 C

Very dry with dark cherry and raspberry-tinged fruit, with a hint of coal. Delicious food wine, chilled.

Stowells of Chelsea Merlot VdP d'Oc (3-litre box)

14 C

Price band has been adjusted to show bottle equivalent.

Stowells Vin de Pays du Gard (3-litre box)

13.5 B

Price band has been adjusted to show bottle equivalent.

Syrah Foncalieu VdP d'Oc 1997

15 C

Good accommodation of tannins with the chewy fruit. Makes for an excellent food wine.

The French Connection Cabernet/Syrah VdP d'Oc 1997

15 C

Curiously it comes on at first like some kind of Chinon but it settles down lushly on the palate to finish with polish. Wine Cellars and Martha's Vineyard only.

VdP de la Vallee du Paradis 1996

15 B

Brilliant value drinking here. Not one whit coarse or over fruity, the wine is dry, characterful, soft, gluggable and food friendly. Great stuff.

FRENCH WINE WHITE

Anjou Blanc, Baud 1997   14   B

Lovely little summer tipple. Has flavour and a vigour of wines costing somewhat more.

Baron Philippe Sauternes 1995 (half bottle)   12   D

Expensive sweetie.

Bordeaux Blanc 1997   13   B

Simple fruity stuff. Most unBordeaux like. More like Henley-on-Thames.

Bordeaux Sauvignon Calvet 1997   12   C

Chablis Domaine de Bieville 1996   14   D

Clean and steely, this is Chablis in its whiplash-fresh and mineral edged mode. A terrific shellfish wine of class.

Chablis Grand Cru, La Chablisienne 1995   10   G

Wine Cellars and Martha's Vineyard only.

Chardonnay VdP d'Oc, Foncalieu 1997   13.5   C

Some decent plumpness about the fruit. Selected stores.

Chateau Eyssards, Bergerac 1997   14 C

A great nutty fish and chicken wine. Terrific Frenchness of fruit. By which I mean the apparent arrogance has real humour underneath.

Chateau La Raz, Montravel 1997   13.5 C

Some hint of the quirkiness of the appellation but it's subtle, very. Wine Cellars and Martha's Vineyard only.

Chateau Tudin Bordeaux 1996   13 D

Clean and crisp.

Colombard/Chardonnay VdP des Cotes de Gascogne, Bouey 1997   14 B

Great fun here. Hints of ripe melon and pineapple.

Domaine de Lions Sauvignon Blanc VdP d'Oc 1997   14 C

Good grassy showiness underlies the gently vegetal fruit.

Fat Bastard Chardonnay VdP d'Oc 1997   15 D

Still fat, still a bastard, still worth keeping nine or twelve months before unloading the fruit (though it's drinkable now).

Fortant Grenache/Chardonnay, VdP d'Oc 1996   15 C

Superb balance of richness and freshness. Has a mineral edge of delicious incisiveness.

French Dry VdP d'Oc, Victoria Wine   13.5 B

French Medium VdP d'Oc, Victoria Wine　　13.5　B

Gewurztraminer, Cave Vinicole de Turckheim 1996　　15　D

James Herrick Chardonnay 1996　　15　C

Good age for a wine not designed to grow old with any great grace. Here it's perfectly mature, melony and lemony and strikes home with style.

La Baume Philippe de Baudin Sauvignon Blanc VdP d'Oc 1997　　16　C

Great class and richness here. A lovely texture, too. It's a seriously well-made sauvignon.

Le Vieux Pont Cotes du Rhone Oaked White 1997　　14.5　C

Good solid fresh water fish wine, at an excellent price. Has real Rhone typicity and style.

Macon-Villages 1996　　13　C

Not bad texture. Has some life and lift to it.

Meursault, Les Chevaliers, Domaine Rene Monnier 1996　　12　G

Great smelly opening but the joke falls flat when there's no punch line. Only at Wine Cellar and Martha's Vineyard stores.

Montagny Premier Cru Oak Aged Chardonnay 1997　　13.5　D

Has a delicious creaminess to the texture. Only at Wine Cellar and Martha's Vineyard stores.

Muscadet Bleu Magnum 1997

Aromatically most posh, unMuscadet-like and positively intriguing. The fruit maintains this promising, fruity debut and the finish is strong and fresh. A wonderful talking point for Christmas lunch. And, empty, the neon blue magnum makes a baseball bat. Price bracket has been adjusted to show the bottle equivalent. Only at Wine Cellar stores.

Muscadet de Sevre et Maine Sur Lie, Domaine de la Roulerie 1997

No, it's not corked. It's Muscadet. Selected stores.

Muscat de Beaumes de Venise, Antoine 1996

A lovely wine for *creme brulee*. Only at Wine Cellar and Martha's Vineyard stores.

Pouilly Fuisse Vieilles Vignes, Domaine de la Soufrandise 1996

Has some plumpness to the texture, which pleases, but the price is also broad-bottomed, and too much so. Only at Wine Cellar and Martha's Vineyard stores.

Pouilly Fume Domaine Herve Seguin 1997

Sancerre Cuvee de Chene de Saint Louis 1996

Sauvignon Blanc, VdP d'Oc 1997

Fine fettle taste bud tickler for the money. Good fish 'n' chip wine.

Stowells of Chelsea VdP du Tarn (3-litre box)

`14` `B`

Price band has been adjusted to show bottle equivalent.

The French Connection Chardonnay/ Viognier VdP d'Oc 1997

`15` `C`

Delicious hints of dry peach and nuts. Wine Cellars and Martha's Vineyard only.

Tokay Pinot Gris, Cave de Turckheim 1997

`13.5` `D`

Good for Thai fish dishes, but needs time. Give it eighteen months, it'll add three points. Wine Cellars and Martha's Vineyard only.

Vouvray Demi-sec Les Coteaux Tufiers 1996

`15` `C`

Lovely richness, dry honey and apricot, and a rich streak of acidity – so it'll age brilliantly. And be great with oriental food.

GERMAN WINE   WHITE

Erdener Treppchen Riesling Kabinett 1986   `15.5` `C`

Kendermann Dry Riesling 1996   `13` `C`

Slate Valley Dry Riesling, Mosel-Saar-Ruwer 1995   `11` `C`

Slate Valley Medium Dry Country Wine 1996   `10` `B`

HUNGARIAN WINE RED

Hidden Rock Reserve Selection Cabernet Sauvignon 1996

An approachable cabernet which doesn't ask a lot of the pocket but then it's undemanding of the palate too. Thus the soft, ripe fruit with its vein of dry tannins is a well priced, highly swallowable composition.

Hungarian Merlot, Danubiana Bonyhad 1997

Possibly the least merlot-like merlot I've ever tasted. Like plum jam. However, with a hot curry, and the wine chilled, you'd have an interesting combination.

HUNGARIAN WINE WHITE

Chapel Hill Rheinriesling 1996

Hidden Rock Gewurztraminer, Mor 1996

A shellfish (Thai inspired) wine of opulent fruitiness which, not classic, is nevertheless fresh and modern.

Hidden Rock Sauvignon Blanc, Sopron 1996

Can't afford Cloudy Bay? Take a trip to Hidden Rock. It's nearer but it's classic sauvignon blanc.

ITALIAN WINE   RED

Amarone delle Valpolicella, Campagnola
1994   `15.5` `E`

Dry, cherryish, figgy and nutty. A fantastic food wine which
though ripe is very tannic and characterful. Lovely stuff. Only
at Wine Cellar and Martha's Vineyard stores.

Argiolas Costera Cannonau di Sardegna
1994   `15.5` `D`

Barbera d'Asti, Icardi 1996   `15` `C`

This has some class to its texture and its finish. The fruit is
well-mannered, dry, with a hint of rich earth, but overall it's
typically Italian in its food friendly versatility and quaffability.

Brunello di Montalcino, Casanova di
Neri 1992   `14` `G`

Wine Cellars and Martha's Vineyard only.

Cabernet Franc San Simone, Friuli 1996   `14.5` `C`

Curious double-act of deliciousness where plum and cherry
fruit, ripe, mingles with a dusty dryness of tannin (light but
positive).

Chianti Classico Rocca di Castignoli 1996   `13.5` `D`

Some cherry ripeness with really rampant, earthy tannins. Needs
time? Perhaps.

Chianti Piccini 1997   `13.5` `C`

Fluid and light with its hint of Tuscany only an echo.

Italian Job Red NV `11` `C`

Montepulciano d'Abruzzo, Cortenova 1996 `14` `C`

Dry cherries and rich earth. Delightful chilled.

**Rosso di Montalcino, Casanova di
Neri 1994** `14.5` `E`

Salice Salento Vallone 1994 `16.5` `C`

Big, brothy, savoury, coffee undertones swirling through a rich,
soft-fruit centre of soft ripeness, this is a lovely glug.

Sangiovese di Toscana Cecchi 1996 `13.5` `C`

Valpolicella 1997 `12` `C`

**Villa Borghetti Valpolicella Classico, Vigneti
in Marano 1995** `13` `C`

**Vino Nobile di Montepulciano, Antica
Chiusina 1991** `15.5` `E`

ITALIAN WINE   WHITE

**Chardonnay/Pinot Grigio Atesino, La
Vis 1996** `15` `C`

Italian Job White NV `11` `C`

Pinot Grigio delle Venezie Ca Donini 1997 `13.5` `C`

Has some attractive nutty undertones.

Soave 1997

Soave Classico Superiore, Zenato 1996

Become ultra chic in your neighbourhood. Serve your friends the most attractive Soave they'll ever taste.

Trebbiano del Romagna Cevico 1997

Nervous, edgy, but great with food: squid stew, for example.

Villa Romana Frascati Superiore 1997

Pretty bland.

MEXICAN WINE RED

Casa Madero Cabernet Sauvignon 1997

Expensive but not on the finish, where it seems woolly. Not at all stores.

MEXICAN WINE WHITE

Casa Madero Chardonnay 1997

When Pancho Villa wasn't shooting Federalis this is what he drank with his bean stew. Such discrimination! Not at all stores.

NEW ZEALAND WINE · RED

Stoneleigh Cabernet Sauvignon 1996 · `13.5` `D`

Very soft and juicy.

NEW ZEALAND WINE · WHITE

Cat's Pee on a Gooseberry Bush Sauvignon/Semillon 1997 · `10` `D`

Still don't like this wine (in its new vintage). It's too vegetally quirky for this old palate.

Cooks Gisborne Chardonnay 1997 · `13` `D`

Corbans Private Bin Chardonnay, Gisborne 1995 · `16` `E`

It's the creamy integration of wood and fruit, which lingers on the taste buds most deliciously, which give the wine its considerable finesse (yet richness). Victoria Wine Cellars only.

Stoneleigh Sauvignon Blanc 1997 · `13` `D`

Not up to previous vintages. Maybe it needs a few more months in bottle (summer 1998).

Villa Maria Private Bin Chardonnay, Marlborough 1997 · `14` `D`

Young (and it will improve) but very rich and ready to provide lingering fruity pleasures.

NEW ZEALAND WHITE

Villa Maria Private Bin Sauvignon Blanc, Marlborough 1997   `16.5` `D`

Superbly greasy grassiness which thunders across the palate with silken hooves; such stealth and purpose here.

PORTUGUESE WINE   RED

Grao Vasco, Dao Vinhos Sogrape 1996   `13` `C`

SOUTH AFRICAN WINE   RED

Boland Wynkelder Merlot/Shiraz 1997   `15.5` `C`

Richly lingering leatheriness and ripeness. Terrific pace to the wine and it doesn't pander to the taste buds – rather it persuades.

Cape View Cinsault/Shiraz 1996   `16` `C`

Great new vintage: soft, subtly spicy with a savoury tang on the finish, lovely warm texture and overall classy. Drinkable and distinguished. Not at all stores.

Cape View Merlot 1997   `15` `C`

Grand little glugging merlot of tenacity, richness and developed finish.

Clearsprings Cape Red NV

10 B

Fruit juice.

Clos Malverne Auret Cabernet
Sauvignon/Pinotage 1996

16 E

Such richness and aplomb must rate well. The exotic edge to the fruit, the positive, well balanced tannins and the flourish on the finish. Very classy stuff. Only at Wine Cellar stores.

Constantia Uitsig Merlot 1996

16 E

Extremely impressive and for a tenner not absurdly priced. The merlot in this specimen is gently peppery, rich, very complex on the finish, dry, smoky, tannic and very classy. Only at Wine Cellar stores.

Delheim Pinotage 1997

 15.5 D

Swinging and bright, dry, peppery, rich and hugely food friendly, this is great quaffing. Only at Wine Cellar stores.

Delheim Shiraz 1997

14 D

Not sure about the hint of poached egg on the fragrance but the fruit is dry, purposeful and richly plummy and well-muscled. Only at Wine Cellar stores.

Long Mountain Cabernet Sauvignon 1997

 13.5 C

Juicy and very ripe.

Louisvale Cabernet Sauvignon/Merlot 1996

15 E

Very stylish and almost regal as it starts work but it does relax and become more demotic, informal and fruity on the finish. This might well be classic Cape cabernet and merlot. Only at Wine Cellar stores.

Mooiplaas Cabernet Sauvignon 1996 `15.5` `E`

In this sort of rich mood, Cape cabernet comes across as the haughtiest of sullen Bordeaux mingled with the raunchiest of sangioveses from fine Classico sites. This implies some delicious tension of styles and the taste buds revel in it. Only at Wine Cellar stores.

Oak Village Cabernet Sauvignon 1996 `15.5` `C`

A deliciously herbal, vegetal (peppers and peas with a hint of cauliflower) and rich, baked, fruity edginess here. A warm, giving cabernet of some class. Only at Wine Cellar stores.

The Pinotage Company Bush Vine Pinotage 1998 `16` `D`

Smells like teenage perfume but the fruit on the taste buds is strict, vegetal, very adult, sensuous and very dry and secure. Stunning glugging, all in all. Only at Wine Cellar stores.

SOUTH AFRICAN WINE WHITE

African Legend Sauvignon Blanc 1998

Perhaps a touch mean of me, this rating, but I can't quite reconcile the frenzy of the exotic fruit with sauvignon. Turkish Delight seems to figure in the finish. Only at Wine Cellar stores.

Agulhas Bank Chardonnay 1996 `15`

Arniston Bay Chenin Blanc/Chardonnay 1998   `13.5` `C`

Very cosmetic-edged and tarty. A bit made up, this wine. Only at Wine Cellar stores.

Boland Colombard 1997   `14` `C`

Very lettuce-crisp and fresh. Delicious, refreshing, striking.

Boland Wynkelder Chardonnay 1997   `13` `C`

Brampton Sauvignon Blanc 1997   `14.5` `D`

Classic grassy sauvignon with New World freshness and concentration. Smashing to drink with smoked fish. Only at Wine Cellar stores.

Cape View Chenin Blanc/Muscat d'Alexandrie, Medium Dry, Paarl 1997   `12.5` `C`

Cape View Chenin/Sauvignon Blanc 1996   `14` `C`

Cape View Colombard, Stellenbosch 1997   `13.5` `C`

Carisbroke Cape White 1998   `16` `B`

Absolutely stunning value here. This is a rich, smoky, hugely flavourful yet balanced, crisp-finishing white of wit and style. Gorgeous stuff at twice the price.

Fairview Semillon 1997   `16.5` `D`

Wonderfully concentrated and freshly turned out. Has great lingering dry peach, vanillary and icy mineral undertones all packed together stylishly and sagely. Utterly delicious wine of class and composure. Not at all stores.

Klein Constantia Sauvignon 1997　　14　E

Classy stuff with a rich concentration of fruit, a hint of grass and hay, and firmness on the finish.

KWV Chardonnay 1997　　13　C

Starts a touch Wagnerish, deep and rolling, and ends up more like something anodyne from Cats (and I don't mean pee).

L'Avenir Chardonnay 1997　　15　E

Very rich finish to the wine, sort of chewy and waxy and tasting of spiced apricots, but overall the fruit, though individual, is a class act. Only at Wine Cellar stores.

Landema Falls Colombard/Chardonnay NV　　14.5　B

Long Mountain Chardonnay 1995　　14.5　C

Long Mountain Chenin Blanc 1996　　13.5　C

Nederburg Chardonnay 1996　　15.5　D

Stowells of Chelsea Chenin Blanc (3-litre box)　　12　B

Price band has been adjusted to show bottle equivalent.

Table Bay Early Release Chenin Blanc 1997　　13.5　C

Van Loveren Pinot Gris 1998　　14.5　C

Love the cork! Comes out like a lump of plasticised slush. But hideous looking as it may be, it's cleaner than any tree bark cork and the fruit is wonderfully preserved, clean and delicious. Only at Wine Cellar stores.

SPANISH WINE   RED

Agramont Tempranillo, Navarra 1996 | 15.5 | C |

Lovely ripe plum texture with tannins, acidity and final fruit flourish in fine, integrated array. Not at all stores.

Campillo Rioja Crianza 1993 | 13.5 | D |

Campo Viejo Rioja Gran Reserva 1993 | 11 | D |

Wrinkly!

Castillo de Liria Valencia NV | 14.5 | B |

Chivite Navarra Vina Marcos 1997 | 13 | C |

Dominio de Montalvo Rioja 1995 | 15.5 | C |

A lovely brisk Rioja with loads of character, flavour and dry but well textured fruit. Modern and hugely quaffable.

Don Darias | 14 | B |

Don Frutos Tempranillo/Cabernet Sauvignon 1996 | 12 | C |

Ed's Red Tempranillo, La Mancha 1996 | 14 | B |

Gran Fuedo Reserva 1994 | 12 | D |

Too sulphurous and ripe for me. Only at Wine Cellar and Martha's Vineyard stores.

La Tasca, Oak Aged, Vino de la Tierra de Manchuela 1996 | 11 | B |

Pago de Carraovejas, Ribera del Duero 1995

`14` `E`

Ripe and raunchy. Expensive and sensual. Only at Wine Cellar and Martha's Vineyard stores.

Retuerta Abadia, Rivola 1996

`16` `D`

Sheer textured class here. Fruit of towering quality and elegant texture, like silk, it's a great investment for the palate which pays off immediately. Only at Wine Cellar and Martha's Vineyard stores.

Roble Tempranillo 1996

`15`

Rich and ripe with lovely earthy tannins. Great with food. Really cuts through food beautifully.

Torre Aldea Rioja 1997

`13.5` `C`

Touch simplistic for four quid.

SPANISH WINE   WHITE

Castillo de Liria Utiel Requena, Valencia NV

`15` `B`

Ed's White 1996

`15` `B`

Lagar de Cervera, Albarino Rias Baixas 1996

`13.5` `D`

Siesta Viura, Vino de la Tierra de Manchuela 1996

`14` `C`

Great fun drinking: from label to throat.

Stowells of Chelsea Viura, Manchuela (3-litre box)

`14` `B`

Price band has been adjusted to show bottle equivalent.

Vinas del Vero Barrel Fermented Chardonnay, Somontano 1996

`16` `D`

Lovely harmony of elements, rich, but with enough zip on the finish to give it a lilting, companionable charm. Wine Cellars and Martha's Vineyard only.

Vinas del Vero Macabeo/Chardonnay, Somontano 1996

`11` `C`

USA WINE   RED

Blossom Hill Californian Red NV

`10` `C`

So light it will disappear without trace with food; without food, what human being lacks the palate to find it other than feeble?

Eagle Peak Merlot 1996

`14.5` `D`

Bit cosy and too much tannin has been lifted out, but it manages, just, to stay the adult side of fruitiness.

USA WINE   WHITE

Blossom Hill NV, California

`10` `C`

Essensia Quady NV (half bottle) `15` `D`

FORTIFIED WINE

Dows Crusted 1991 `16` `F`

A gorgeous Christmas present: rich, deep, figgy and not oversweet.

Dows LBV 1992 `13.5` `F`

Sweet and fruit-cakey.

Grahams Malvedos 1984 `13.5` `G`

Quinta de Vargellas Vintage Port 1986 `15` `G`

What vintage port is all about. It cobbles together richness and sweetness with hugely lingering depth of positiveness. Wine Cellar stores only.

Taylors Quinta de Terra Feita 1986 `15` `G`

Taylors Vintage Port 1985 `13` `H`

Warres Traditional LBV 1984 `15` `G`

SPARKLING WINE/CHAMPAGNE

Asti Perlino (Italy) `13` `C`

Blossom Hill Sparkling NV (USA) | 11 | D |

Good for geriatrics whose teeth are not all sweet.

Cava Brut NV | 15 | C |

Brilliant value for money.

Charles Courbet Champagne NV | 15.5 | F |

An excellently structured Champagne of classic toasty overtones yet pert dry finishing power. A bargain under a tenner.

Cuvee Napa Brut, Mumm NV | 15 | E |

Cuvee Napa Rose, Mumm NV | 14 | E |

Deutz (New Zealand) | 15.5 | E |

Graham Beck Brut (South Africa) | 13 | D |

Jacques Monteau Champagne Brut NV | 12 | F |

Lanson Brut Rose (France) | 10 | H |

Lindauer Brut | 13.5 | D |

Marquis de la Tour Brut (France) | 13 | C |

Marquis de la Tour Demi Sec NC (France) | 8 | C |

A touch revolting.

Marquis de la Tour Millennium Blend (France) | 16 | D |

Brilliant value for money. Dry, hint of fruit, positive finish.

Marquis de la Tour Rose NV (France) · 14 · C

Nothing wrong with this for a penny change out of four quid. It's dry and stylish.

Mercier Brut Rose NV (France) · 12 · G

Millennium Grand Cru Brut Champagne 1990 · 12 · H

Moet et Chandon Brut 1992 · 10 · H

Pinot/Chardonnay Frizzante, Pasqua (Italy) · 10 · C

Pol Roger White Foil · 11 · H

Prosecco, La Marca (Italy) · 14 · C

Rotari Brut Mezzacorona NV · 10 · D

Somewhat cloddish.

Seaview Brut Rose · 14 · D

If you like avuncular charm and a hint of English strawberry, this is an aperitif for you.

Seppelt Sparkling Shiraz 1993 · 15 · E

Veuve Clicquot La Grande Dame 1989 · 13 · H

WINE CELLAR

BARGAIN BUY OF THE DECADE? OR AN IMPOSSIBLE DREAM?

Last year, Greenalls Cellars (a 460-strong northern off licence chain) sold its shops to a management buyout team, called Parisa, led by chief executive Nader Haghighi for £56 million. Mr Haghighi's precise share of the business was, and is, not known (and is, frankly, none of my business either), but the current management team, it was reported, are 'likely to become very wealthy' if the business continues to grow at its current rate. The report in *The Times* newspaper, which loves stories like this, said that Mr Haghighi, now 38, used to sell cigarettes and chewing gum on the streets of Iran as a child.

Parisa immediately upon acquisition re-opened 12 of these 460 stores under a Booze Buster fascia with the stated aim of under-cutting the supermarkets by 30%. There were plans, so I was told, to open a further 50 and extend the idea further through franchising. Locations for the first Booze Busters included Blackpool, Crewe, Stoke-on-Trent, Wrexham and Warrington. Parisa also opened three Wine Cellars outlets in the south-east – at Reading, East Grinstead and East Sheen. All three with the in-store cafés already seen in other Wine Cellars outlets.

Earlier this year, the company announced that some 50 new stores were going to open as part of a £10 million investment programme. The bulk of this investment was to be spent on Booze Buster but money will also be used to expand Wine Cellars shops in the south-east.

Parisa then announced plans to open a chain of specialist beer shops with their own micro-breweries, an idea which coincides with Victoria Wine's Firkin Off Licences which sell cask beer brewed at Firkin breweries. The company also announced that half-yearly trading profits were up 15% on last year – £4.3million was the quoted figure.

For the wine drinker, the only true innovative idea which comes out of this is that in a Wine Cellar with a café it is possible to buy wine off the shelf in the shop and drink it in the café. This avoids the vast mark-up which restaurants scandalously and routinely apply to their wines as a means of subsidising the kitchen (or more likely to fund either the chef's expensive life-style or to mitigate the crippling conditions of the crazy lease) and so there is a bonus here. I plan to eat in a Wine Cellar soon and report on the experience. The idea of the wine shop/café is an excellent one and this is the only aspect of Parisa's business which sets it apart from other wine shops or supermarket wine departments (which it cannot really hope to compete with in the long term).

The shelves of wines at Wine Cellar hold several gems. As the listing which follows demonstrates. These are mainly in the middling to expensive price brackets. The company does little, if any, innovation in the pure wine sense or in the way that the supermarkets and large wine chains do it. It uses suppliers' already packaged wines and I would assume that some of these suppliers make contributions, as is normal, to the marketing overheads of pushing their wines in store. The wine buying department, the brave Mr David Vaughan coping manfully, does not initiate projects to create wines because he hasn't the staff or the impetus. I sometimes wonder if he doesn't feel a little constricted.

The business's focus, as a retailer, is with expansion and increasing turnover through this. This need not necessarily be a bad thing if the wine range, like say Oddbins', is of great depth and originality and has lots of wines unavailable elsewhere. I can't, however, help the feeling that, unlike say Majestic where a love of and furious enthusiasm for wine permeates the whole company, here there is a more hard-headed business approach which is energised by jumping on established bandwagons, calling the odd one innovative because it sounds impressive, and hoping that the bullish mood of wine drinkers will simply drive the business to greater and greater profitability. Well, the half-year figures above patently show that this is one way to do it, but what happens if there's a slump or if the competition makes expansion too expensive? The plan is one day to float the whole shebang and for the directors and other shareholders to make a small fortune, I presume.

This latter consideration holds no excitement or interest for me whatsoever (unless a merger took place to infuse it). All I care about is my readers getting terrific wines at the right prices. Mr Vaughan does as good a job as he can, but shouldn't he have more freedom, more money, more resources to develop the wine range?

Wine Cellar (Parisa Limited)
P O Box 476
Loushers Lane
Warrington
Cheshire WA4 6RQ
Tel: 01925 444555
Fax: 01925 415474
e-mail: gf95@dial.pipex.com

ARGENTINIAN WINE

RED

Balbi Vineyard Cabernet Sauvignon 1996

15.5 | C

La Rural Merlot 1997

15.5 | C

Juicy and ripe, oh yes all the modern appurtenances are here, but the marmite of soupiness herein displayed has a backlash of flavour on the finish which hints at some depth and character.

Libertad Sangiovese Malbec 1997

14 | C

Sheer lovely juice, but at this price it's acceptable juice.

Norton Barbera 1996

15 | C

The sense of purpose – to provide sheer pleasure – runs through every drop of this fruit. It's positive and enchanting.

Norton Malbec 1996

14 | C

Juicy and cheroot-edged.

Norton Privada 1996

16.5 | E

Love its rich flamboyance and concentration. Like a breath of Buenos Aires night life.

Norton Sangiovese 1996

15 | C

Makes many a Chianti seem not only archaic but austere. Clods of fruit here.

Rafael Estate Tempranillo 1997

14 | C

Again that Argentine hallmark: runaway jamminess with a hint of worldliness.

Santa Julia Pinot Noir 1997 | 13 | C

Not entirely convincing.

Valle de Vistalba Cabernet Sauvignon 1995 | 14 | C

Very perky and alert with some tannic savouriness to the fruit.

Valle de Vistalba Syrah 1996 | 13.5 | C

ARGENTINIAN WINE · WHITE

Balbi Chardonnay 1997 | 14.5 | C

Ripe and very richly engaging. Would be wonderful with that old Loire dish of chicken and endives.

Balbi Syrah Rose 1996 | 14 | C

La Rural Chardonnay 1997 | 15 | C

Has softness with a gentle pineapple and melon edge. Needs fish to show itself to best advantage.

Libertad Chenin 1997 | 15 | C

Clean and fresh with a hint of hay and nuts. This is a bargain chenin for food.

Valle de Vistalba Chardonnay 1997 | 13 | C

Touch muted and ho-hum on the finish.

AUSTRALIAN WINE RED

Baileys Block 1920 Shiraz 1995 `16` `E`

Great tannins and textured richness. Why can't more Aussies make ten quid wine so adult and sensual?

Baileys Shiraz 1995 `15` `D`

Improving nicely in bottle. The maker understands tannin and the character it can bequeath to wine.

Bests Victoria Cabernet 1994 `13` `E`

Juice, pure juice (with a hint of attitude).

Capel Vale Shiraz 1996 `16` `E`

Trust Western Australia to enhance the Aussie's reputation. This is not the usual soppy shiraz, soft as a sponge and half as characterful, yet it still has that unique savoury aroma and texture of first class Aussie shiraz. However, what it's got in addition is a dry, herby, slightly Rhone edge to it – so it has some guts. It's immensely quaffable and also good with food.

Grant Burge Cabernet Sauvignon 1995 `14` `E`

Lot of money but a load of fruit. A wheel barrow full of it, all ripe, soft and jammy. Good curry wine.

Grant Burge Old Vine Shiraz 1995 `14` `F`

Very soft and juicy but the hint of tannin on the finish saves it from soppiness.

Hardys Bankside Shiraz 1996 `14` `D`

Has some ruggedness to its essentially easy-going character.

Lindemans Bin 45 Cabernet Sauvignon 1996 `14` `D`

Juicy and jammy but the tannins buttress this softness and ripeness properly.

Penfolds Rawson's Retreat Bin 35 Cabernet/Shiraz 1996 `15.5` `D`

Rich, layered, clinging, ripe – a great steak and kidney pudding wine.

Peter Lehmann Vine Vale Grenache 1997 `14.5` `C`

Sticky fruit of great adhesive character where food is concerned. Hums with fruit.

Rosemount Estate Cabernet Sauvignon 1996 `14.5` `D`

Big, juicy, rich.

Rosemount Grenache Shiraz 1997 `13.5` `D`

More Aussie juice.

Taltarni Fiddleback Terrace 1996 `14` `E`

Very ripe and raisiny to the extent that the tannins cower in some fright. Needs food.

AUSTRALIAN WINE WHITE

Hardys Padthaway Chardonnay 1996 `16` `E`

Do you like Meursault? You'll like this, then. This kind of

woody, hay-rich, vegetal fruitiness is a miracle under eight quid.

Ironstone Semillon Chardonnay 1997 | 15.5 | D

A rich, dry, crisp food wine of compelling double-faced furtiveness. It shows one side of itself which is soft and almost creamily fruity and then a crisp, raw delicious fresh face.

Lindemans Bin 70 Semillon/Verdelho/Sauvignon Blanc/Chardonnay 1997 | 15 | D

Brilliant soft spiciness for oriental food.

Penfolds Rawson's Retreat Bin 21 Semillon/Chardonnay/Colombard 1997 | 15 | C

Nice exotic edge, not overbaked, which mingles well with the minerally acidity. Good food wine.

Rosemount Semillon Chardonnay 1997 | 15 | D

Elegant and worldly. Serve it with grilled white fish.

Taltarni Fiddleback Terrace 1996 | 12 | E

Too much money by far.

CHILEAN WINE   RED

Aguirre Palo Alto Merlot 1997 | 13 | C

Very vegetal.

Mapocho Merlot 1997 | 14.5 | C

Has delicious savoury depths with a hint of tobacco.

CHILEAN RED

Vino de Chile Talca 15 B

CHILEAN WINE WHITE

Andes Peaks Sauvignon Blanc 1997 15 C

Excellent varietal character with hints of gooseberry, raspberry
and nuts. Delicious aperitif.

FRENCH WINE RED

Boisset Bourgogne Pinot Noir 1996 12.5 D

Lot of money for the level of excitement generated.

**Chateau Beausejour Cotes de Castillon
1996** 14 C

Rather juicy for a Claret and the vegetality is subsumed under
this fruitiness but it finishes well.

Chateau Fortia Chateauneuf-du-Pape 1994 17.5 F

Expensive but tremendous. It's classic CduP with its texture,
ripeness yet depth of seriousness and gripping tannins. The
complexity is wide, deep and lingering.

Chateau Paloumey Haut-Medoc 1993 15 E

Expensive treat with its soupy richness, lightly framed by
tannins, and positive textured finish.

Cote du Ventoux Domaine de la Peyronniere 1996 `14.5` `C`

Pleasant, fruity, simple, not remotely earthy or rustic except in a faraway echo of Provence on the teeth after the wine has quit the throat.

L'Enclos des Cigales Corbieres 1995 `15` `C`

March Hare Red d'Oc 1996 `16` `C`

Svelte, rich, smooth, engaging, worldly, handsome, polite – under a fiver this is a real charmer.

No Bull Cabernet/Merlot d'Oc 1996 `15.5` `C`

Wonderful little cab: gets you from nose to throat in great comfort with gently peppery fruitiness.

Port Neuf Rouge `13` `B`

FRENCH WINE WHITE

Boisset Bourgogne Chardonnay 1996 `13` `D`

No Bull Grenache Blanc/Chardonnay 1996 `11` `C`

Port Neuf White `14.5` `B`

Wild Trout White 1997 `15` `C`

Has a classy nervousness of fruity gentility which contrasts nicely with the unrestrained immediacy of the acidity.

ITALIAN WINE   RED

Barbera d'Asti Fondatori 1993   14   D

Very nervous fruit, edge and rich, and great with food.

Barbera la Castagnola 1996   14   C

A tombstone of a wine (celebrating the Marchesa of 1811) but
the fruit is lively, soft, ripe and modern.

Copertino Rosso Riserva 1993   14.5 C

---

d'Istinto Sangiovese/Merlot 1997 (Sicily)   15.5 C

Great gobbets of earthy rich tannins. Gorgeous bristly fruit here.
Great for food.

Duca di Castelmonte Cent'are Rosso
1996 (Sicily)   15   C

Soft and jammy with rich ripe tannins. Great glugging here.

ITALIAN WINE   WHITE

Bianco Cent'are Duca di Castelmonte 1997   14.5 C

A wonderful Italian foodie! It's quiet yet rich, firm yet soft,
palate-pleasing yet with the serious intention to marry fish.

Chardonnay La Castagnola 1996 `14` `C`

Very rich and full of itself yet not boring company.

Langhe Chardonnay 1996 `15` `C`

Superb polish and manners here. Quite posh as it finishes. Not quite a plum in its mouth but definitely a small melon.

Puglian Bianco Cantele, Kim Milne `13` `C`

NEW ZEALAND WINE RED

Esk Valley Cabernet//Merlot 1995 `14` `E`

NEW ZEALAND WINE WHITE

Oyster Bay Sauvignon Blanc 1997 `16` `D`

Gorgeous ripeness with ripe melon, grass, asparagus and Brazil nuts all cobbled together in sensual array.

PORTUGUESE WINE RED

Alianca Palmela Paticular 1992 `14` `D`

Very calm and polished. Almost smug.

Portada Tinto Estremadura 1995 · 16 · C

Great value here. An aromatic, gorgeously soft, rich, ripe wine with a walloping fruity finish.

Quinta do Vale da Raposa 1995 · 15 · D

Ripe and rich, good earthy edge, and an accomplished finish.

ROMANIAN WINE · RED

Pietroasa Young Vatted Cabernet Sauvignon 1996 · 15.5 · C

Delicious chirpy, cheeky brew smelling and tasting of gently peppery blackcurrant, as cab. sauv. is classically supposed to. But underlying it is warmth and personality.

SOUTH AFRICAN WINE · RED

First River Winery Stellenbosch Dry Red · 14 · C

SPANISH WINE · RED

Enate Crianza Tempranillo/Cabernet 1995 · 16.5 · D

Gorgeous aromatic fruit of a lovely balance of elements offering richness, texture and a great clinging finish. A classy wine of great style.

Glorioso Crianza Rioja 1995 · 15.5 · D

Modern and soft, good richness of attack (not overbaked or furiously woody) and it finishes elegantly.

La Prensa Tempranillo La Mancha 1997 · 16 · C

Brilliant value here with ripe plum/blackcurrant fruit beautifully riddled with tannins.

Vinas del Vero Cabernet Sauvignon 1995 · 15 · C

SPANISH WINE — WHITE

Vinas del Vero Chardonnay 1996 · 13.5 · C

SWISS WINE — RED

Pinot Noir Trilogy 1996 · 12 · D

Light, but not light on the pocket.

SWISS WINE — WHITE

Chasselas Trilogy 1996 · 15.5 · C

Unusual dry apricot fruit – soft/crisp texture, vegetal undertone, hint of cream – it's unusual all right.

Fendant du Valais Blanc 1996 — `15.5` `D`

Deliciously different! A wine to turn you off chardonnay and on to less mannered fruit where the theme is restraint, elegance and a witty finish. It taste clean and mountainous.

Les Grands Dignitaires Pinot Blanc/ Chardonnay Valais 1996 — `16` `E`

Quirky and polished with ripe melon and fresh acidity beautifully blended in a gust of flavour which is always full of finesse.

USA WINE — RED

Clos du Val: Le Clos NV — `14` `E`

Very ripely textured, but there is a comforting sense of fun and sun to the wine plus an earthy edge to give it some backbone.

Fetzer Pinot Noir, Santa Barbara 1996 — `13` `D`

An echo of the sinful exoticism which pinot noir can attain. But seven quid for the echo is a mite much even though the wine is respectable (but we crave indecency!).

Firesteed Pinot Noir 1993 — `14` `E`

Paul Thomas Cabernet/Merlot 1995 — `14` `E`

Interesting richness to the fruit. Has some character and bite. Overall, a polished, if not gripping, performance.

Saddle Mountain Grenache 1994 — `13.5` `C`

STOP PRESS

MAJESTIC

AUSTRALIAN WINE — WHITE

Yenda Chardonnay 1998

Remarkably multi-layered and fruit salad-like without being puerile. It combines melon, pear, pineapple and apple.

Yenda Semillon Chardonnay 1998

Very full and forward, juicy and thick, but with oriental food it should prove a versatile and amusing companion.

CHILEAN WINE — RED

Tocornal Chilean Red 1998

Terrific dryness yet fruity charm here. Comes across like an old softie in a knitted cardigan at first taste, then it reveals itself as a hip character in a soft leather suit.

CHILEAN WINE — WHITE

Tocornal Chilean White 1998

With its handsome healthy plastic cork the fruit is delivered fresh and flavoursome: apples, underripe melon and a touch of pineapple. Lovely stuff!

SPANISH WINE   RED

Costers del Gravet, Tarragona 1996   16.5   E

Very ripe and rich, beautiful tannins giving balance to both fruit and alcohol (13.5%) and this priorat-style wine is polished yet rustic with hints of fig and raisin. A marvellous blend of cab, gar and car (you work it out).

Mas Collet Tarragona 1996   16.5   C

A superbly vigorous blend of garnacha, tempranillo, carinena and cabernet sauvignon. Here is texture, perfume, fruit, litheness yet weight, and great gobbets of hedgerow flavours – plus a hint of hillside herbs. Wonderful soupy, savoury finish.

Muga Rioja Reserva 1994   16   E

This has improved stunningly in bottle since I tasted it earlier this year (c.f. the entry in the main section of the book). The tannins and fruit are bruisers of welter-weight class and punch with style. Rugged, old-fashioned and grizzly but not remotely cosmetic or vanillary.

SPANISH WINE   WHITE

Martin Codax Albarino Rias Baixas 1997   15   D

That curious sticky-toffee edge and apple/melon undertone to nutty fruit is a peculiarity of this Galician white. An acquired taste? Not really. It makes a change from chardonnay even if you only get a penny change out of six quid. A wonderful wine to drink with radishes.

USA WINE   WHITE

Fetzer Viognier 1996   15.5   E

ODDBINS

AUSTRALIAN WINE   RED

Tatachilla Foundation McLaren Vale
Shiraz 1996   15   F

A big soupy dry broth-complex wine with subdued spice and
vegetality but a very rich baked earthy fruitiness of some charm
– even if this charm is far from subtle. It needs food of similar
energy and exuberant richness.

AUSTRALIAN WINE   WHITE

Peter Lehmann Eden Valley Riesling 1997   15.5   D

Sherbety riesling of rich classiness and texture, improving nicely
in bottle (c.f. the entry for this wine in the main Oddbins section
of the book).

CHILEAN WINE   RED

Casablanca Santa Isabel Estate Cabernet
Sauvignon 1997   17   E

Has such dry depth but, paradoxically, with such weepiness

of cassis-edged fruit that the drinker is deliciously puzzled. Ravishing now, I rather fancy it will over eighteen months develop coffee and tobacco manners.

Casablanca Santa Isabel Estate Merlot 1997

Unusually minty and very dry merlot, not especially typical but then neither is it cliched. It is very beautifully textured, a touch taut, and highly concentrated.

GREEK WINE   RED

Mavrodaphne of Patras NV (50 cl)

A spicy, brick-red pudding wine – cloves, cinnamon, and blackcurrants – which with Christmas cake would be sublime.

GREEK WINE   WHITE

Tselepos Moschofilero, Mantinia 1997

15   D

Is developing some interesting chewy quirkiness in bottle (c.f. the entry in the main Oddbins section of the book), with delicious apple-skin fruitiness.

SOUTH AFRICAN WINE   RED

Blaauwklippen Shiraz 1997   14   D

Remarkably fruity and fulsome with a hint of dry fig and cassis on the finish. It cries out for food.

Savanha Cabernet Sauvignon 1997   16   D

Brilliant vegetality and cabernet correctness. Solid and excitingly packed with fruit.

SPANISH WINE   RED

Espival Tempranillo Somontano 1997   15   C

Astonishingly Aussie-like in feel and flavour with its puppy-dog soft fruit and savoury richness. An interesting companion for pastas and ungainly casseroles.

La Cata Tempranillo La Mancha 1997   14   B

Gravy-like richness on the finish makes the wine meaty and unfussy.

USA WINE   WHITE

Ca' de Solo Bloody Good Pink 1997   15   D

Raspberry ripple ice cream meets pineapple sorbet – plus alcohol. A marvellous rose for warm weather suppers.

THRESHER

ARGENTINIAN WINE WHITE

Norton Torrontes, Mendoza 1997

Brilliant food wine: loads of flavour and strength of purpose.

AUSTRALIAN WINE RED

Deakin Estate Victoria Merlot 1997

Terrific price for such savourily rich, ripe, gently spicy fruit. Yes, it's soft and approachable but there's personality and bite here too. Wine Rack only.

BULGARIAN WINE WHITE

Sauvignon Blanc Domaine Boyar, Targovischte 1997

Whistle clean, biting, classy edges. And its plastic cork means no cork taint!

ITALIAN WINE
RED

Autunno Sangiovese di Puglia NV

Delicious old world earthiness meets new world softness and direct charm. A terrific pasta plonk.

ITALIAN WINE
WHITE

Portabello Vina da Tavola NV

Chewy and bright, bit bland on the finish but this quibble means nothing in the context of a drinks party.

ROMANIAN WINE
WHITE

River Route Limited Edition Chardonnay 1997

Gently lemonic, hint of vegetality, soft texture.

VICTORIA WINE

ARGENTINIAN WINE   RED

Las Lilas Malbec Syrah 1997   `16` `C`

This is improving magnificently in bottle (c.f. the entry in the main Victoria Wine section of this book) and now offers lovely charcoal-rich, chewy fruit of dryness yet warm wryness. Terrific glug with wide food-matching possibilities.

AUSTRALIAN WINE   RED

Hardys Mills Cellars Grenache 1997   `15` `D`

Aussie red wine lover's dream meets the Rhone ranger's favourite finish. Thus we have jammy savouriness, richness, and enough character for food.

AUSTRALIAN WINE   WHITE

Hardys Mills Cellars Chardonnay 1997   `16` `D`

Relaxed wine, it unfolds gently yet purposefully its delicious plan of action: first vanilla, then pear, then melon, then a hint of cream – then it rushes to embrace the throat. Great charm!

Hardys Mills Cellars Semillon 1997 | 14 | D |

Nicely stick-to-your-gums semillon of richness and texture. Great with a fried chunk of swordfish.

CHILEAN WINE   RED

Errazuriz Don Maximiano Founder's Reserve 1994 | 17 | F |

Reserved yes but mightily exuberant; rich, deep and so finely textured yet characterful it seems an alien construct.

La Palma Cabernet/Merlot 1997 | 16.5 | C |

So sublimely tasty and unfussy, unpretentious and inexpensive, that it creates the critical conditions by which we are forced to judge it. It combines leather and cassis, youthfully and with wit.

Santa Rita 120 Cabernet Sauvignon 1996 | 15.5 | C |

Rich, ripe, not remotely peppery and uptight, but a relaxed, soft, calmly drinkable specimen of savouriness and style.

CHILEAN WINE   WHITE

Altura Chardonnay 1997 | 15.5 | C |

Rich, melony, hint of sour butter – delicious and very modern.

FRENCH WINE   RED

Abbotts Cumulus Shiraz 1997 | 15.5 | | C |

The impressive fruit of the '96 is not quite so powerfully in evidence in the '97. Abbotts is herby, rich, dry and characterful and with a deft balance of elements providing class and substance. This is more playful and soft than the '96.

Fortant de France Syrah/Cabernet Sauvignon d'Oc 1996 | 14.5 | | C |

Earthily rich and ripe but stays the civilised side of rustic.

FRENCH WINE   WHITE

Chardonnay VdP du Jardin de la France 1997 | 14 | | C |

Better than most Muscadets next door.

Chateau La Tuque Bordeaux 1997 | 14.5 | | C |

Clean, crisp, fresh, modern yet with a hint of old Bordeaux blanc on the finish.

Laperriere Chardonnay VdP du Jardin de la France 1997 | 14.5 | | C |

Crisp and steely with hints of underripe melon. Good fish wine. Subdued but classy.

ITALIAN WINE RED

Pieve della Fontana Rosso di Toscana 1995 [14.5] [E]

Rather a haughty red with rustic touches. A wine to drink whilst reading Tomasi di Lampedusa.

PORTUGUESE WINE RED

Terra Boa Vinho Tinto 1997 [14] [C]

Delicious cherry/blackcurrant fruit with a hint of earth.

SPANISH WINE RED

Senorio de Robles Jumilla 1997 [15.5] [B]

It's the texture which makes it so appealing and character-laden. Has hints of tobacco and plum to the fruit.

SPANISH WINE WHITE

Rioja Montalvo Limited Edition 1995 [14] [D]

Woody and somewhat chewy, this wine calls for food of richness and spiciness.